new jewish tunes.

ruach 5767 songbook

includes CD (also available separately)

Editors
Michael Boxer
Jayson Rodovsky

Typesetter
Eric S. Komar

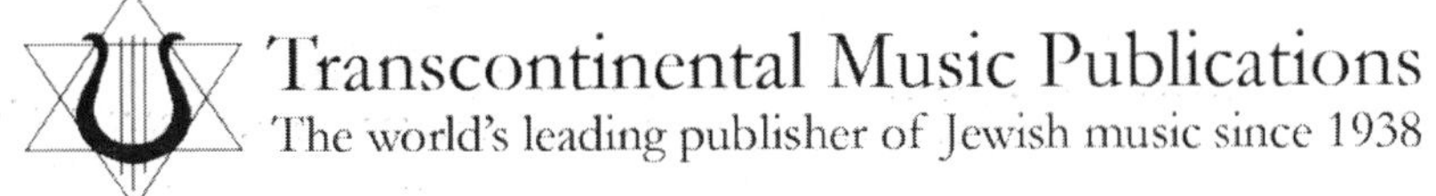

Visit **www.RuachCD.com**

for artist information, educational material, and downloads

Hebrew Pronunciation Guide

VOWELS

a as in *father*

ai as in *aisle* (= long *i* as in *ice*)

e = short *e* as in *bed*

ei as in *eight* (= long *a* as in *ace*)

i as in *pizza* (= long *e* as in *be*)

o = long *o* as in *go*

u = long *u* as in *lunar*

' = unstressed vowel close to ə or unstressed short *e*

CONSONANTS

ch as in German *Bach* or Scottish *loch* (not as in *cheese*)

g = hard *g* as in **get** (not soft *g* as in **gem**)

tz = as in *boats*

h after a vowel is silent

Ruach 5767 Songbook: New Jewish Tunes

CD Executive Committee: Hope Chernak, Rabbi Michael Mellen, and Jayson Rodovsky
Executive Producer : Michael Boxer

A division of the Union for Reform Judaism
633 Third Avenue - New York, NY 10017 - Fax 212.650.4119
212.650.4105 - **www.TranscontinentalMusic.com** - tmp@urj.org
993314

Manufactured in the United States of America
Cover design by Pine Point Productions - Windham, ME
Book design by Joel N. Eglash
Additional design by Michael Boxer
ISBN 8074-1076-4
10 9 8 7 6 5 4 3 2 1

Preface

Ruach is the Hebrew word for *spirit*. It is exactly *that* quality which the songs of the *Ruach* series possess. These songs were chosen for their ear-catching melodies, their colorful instrumental support, and for the life the music breathes into their texts. In short, all this is summed up by one common trait: *ruach*.

The *Ruach* series is the continuation of the seven original NFTY (North American Federation of Temple Youth) albums that were recorded between 1972 and 1989 (see the NFTY five-CD set available from Transcontinental Music). The NFTY and *Ruach* albums are primary sources of participatory music for cantors, songleaders, musical leaders and all those who disseminate Jewish music. Through their leadership, the tradition of singing is passed on to the next generation of campers and youth groupers: the future songleaders, cantors, and musical leaders. This songbook is another way of preserving this musical tradition for future generations.

Joel N. Eglash
Series Creator

Thanks are due to Loui Dobin, Lauren Dubin, Joel N. Eglash, Rabbi Dan Freelander, Melissa Goldman, Eric Komar, Victor Ney, Melissa Zalkin Stollman, Rachel Wetstein, Cantor Rosalie Will-Boxt, the members of the *Ruach 5767* committee, whose varying backgrounds and experiences helped shape this remarkable collection of music; and, of course, the artists who have created this great music for all of us.

RUACH 5767 COMMITTEE

Michael Boxer
Hope Chernak
Adrian Durlester
Seth Gordon-Lipkin
Cantor Alane Katzew
Zack Kolstein
Rabbi Michael Mellen
Rabbi Hara Person
Dr. Jayson Rodovsky

table of contents

ruach 5767

ruach 5767
songbook

on 1 foot by sheldon low

text & music: sheldon low & rick recht, based on sifra: k'doshim

> My Dad is a great storyteller, and one of my favorite stories of his is about the man who asked Hillel to teach him the whole Torah while standing on one foot. Hillel responded with, "What is hateful to you, do not do to another." Several years back, a woman asked me to sum up all of Judaism in a few sentences, to which I replied, "I can tell you a story ..."

Hard rock (♩= 158)

Intro

G Am7 G/B Em
Hal - le - lu - - - yah, sing hal -

D G Am7 G/B Em
- le - lu - yah. Hal - le - lu - yah, sing ha -

D VI G Am7
le - lu - yah. To the house came a man. "On one

G/B C G
foot," he asked Hil - lel, "can you teach me ev - 'ry-thing?"

Am7 G/B Em D
Hil - lel said, "All you got - ta do is"

Ch
G Am7 G/B Em
Treat one an - oth - er as your friend. Sis - ter and
Hal - le - lu - - - yah, sing hal -
D G Am7
broth - er in the end. Treat one an - oth - er as your friend.
- le - lu - yah. Hal - le - lu - - - yah,
G/B Em
1.
D
V2
G
Sis - ter and broth - er in the end.
In our lives we will meet
sing hal - le - lu - yah.
Am7 G/B C G
so man-y peo - ple who are dif - f'rent. We must treat them as we'd have oth -
Am7 G/B Em D
- ers treat us. I'll say it a - gain: All you got - ta do is

2.
Br
D
C
Hil - lel said to that man stand - ing there
broth - er in the end.
- le - lu - yah.

G
on one foot, "Hang in there, friend, as long as you can. I'll

Am7
3
Em
D
put it to you sim - ple so you'll tru - ly un - der - stand."

End
Cadd9
G/B
Treat one an - oth - er as your friend.

1.-3.
4.
Am7sus4
G/B
Em
Sis - ter and broth - er in the end. broth - er in the end.

Hal - le - lu - yah, sing hal - le - lu - yah.

G
Am7
G/B
Em
Treat one an - oth - er as your friend.
Sis - ter and
Hal - le - lu - - - yah,
sing hal -
D
Repeat 5 times
G
Am7
broth - er in the end.
- le - lu - yah.
Hal - le - lu - - - yah,
G/B
Em
D
G
Hal - le - lu - yah.
sing hal - le - lu - yah.

l'dor vador by dan nichols

from generation to generation

hebrew: liturgy (amidah)
music: dan nichols

> Dan's rendition of this prayer has become part of the NFTY-ites' culture of *T'filah.* It just seems to speak to their hearts. As a spiritual leader, as a rock musician, he really connects with them. Watching the kids sing this song at Kutz Camp with such *Ruach* and commitment, with their arms around each other, was always such a moving experience. -- *Hope Chernak*

Passionately (♩= 85)

capo 3: *Em* Gm — *Bm7* Dm7 — *Cadd9* E♭add9 — *D* F — *Em* Gm — *Bm7* Dm7

(Instrumental)

Cadd9 E♭add9 — *D* F — V — *Em* Gm — *Bm7* Dm7 — *Cadd9* E♭add9 — *D* F — *Em* Gm — *Bm7* Dm7

L' dor va - dor na-gid god - le-cha

Cadd9 E♭add9 — *D* F — *Em* Gm — *Bm7* Dm7 — *Cadd9* E♭add9 — *D* F

u - l'-nei - tzach n' - tza-chim k'-du-shat-

Em Gm — *Bm7* Dm7 — *Cadd9* E♭add9 — *D* F — *Em* Gm — *Bm7* Dm7

- cha nak - dish. L'-dor va - dor

Cadd9 E♭add9 — *D* F — *Em* Gm — *Bm7* Dm7 — *Cadd9* E♭add9 — *D* F

na - gid god - le - cha u - l'-nei-

Em Gm — *Bm7* Dm7 — *Cadd9* E♭add9 — *D* F — To Coda — *Em* Gm — *Bm7* Dm7 — *Cadd9* E♭add9 — *D* F

- tzach n' - tza chim k' du-shat - cha nak - dish.

Ch
G Bb D F Eb° F#°
V' - shiv - cha - cha, E - lo - hei - nu, mi -
Em Gm C Eb Cm Ebm
pi - nu lo ya - mush l' - o - lam va - ed.
G Bb D F Eb° F#°
V' - shiv - cha - cha, E - lo - hei - nu, mi -
Em Gm A7 C7
pi - nu lo ya - mush l' - o - lam va - ed, l' - o -
1.
Am Cm tacit Em Gm Bm7 Dm7
lam va - ed.
Cadd9 Ebadd9 D F Em Gm Bm7 Dm7 Cadd9 Ebadd9 D F
L' dor va -
2.
Am Cm Br E G
lam va - ed. Ba - ruch A - tah, A - do - nai,
Am Cm E G
A - do - nai. Ba - ruch A - tah,

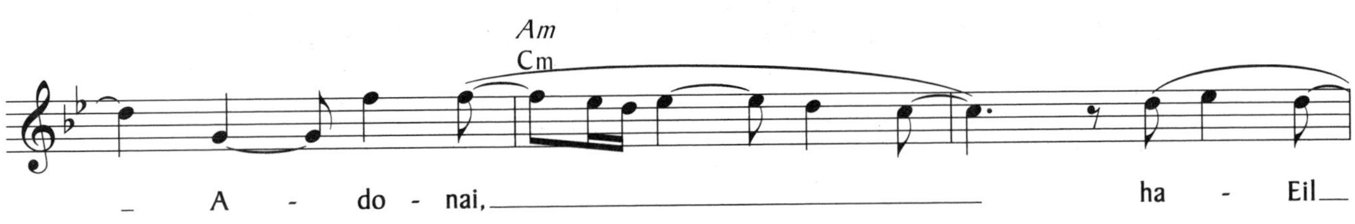

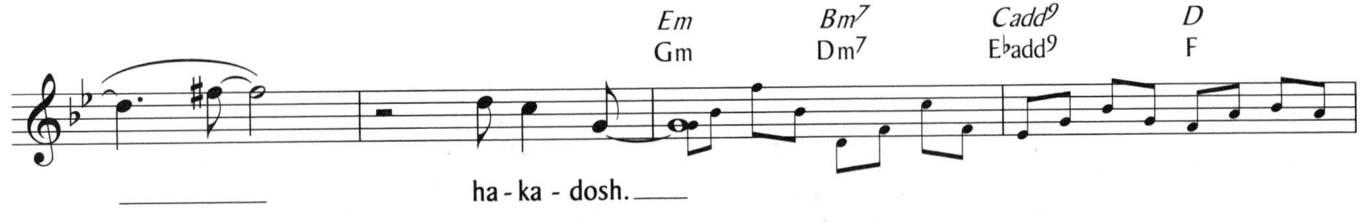

לְדוֹר וָדוֹר נַגִּיד גָּדְלֶךָ וּלְנֵצַח נְצָחִים
קְדֻשָּׁתְךָ נַקְדִּישׁ. וְשִׁבְחֲךָ, אֱלֹהֵינוּ,
מִפִּינוּ לֹא יָמוּשׁ לְעוֹלָם וָעֶד.
בָּרוּךְ אַתָּה, יְיָ, הָאֵל הַקָּדוֹשׁ.

To all generations we will make known Your greatness, and to all eternity proclaim Your holiness. Your praise, O God, shall never depart from our lips. Blessed are You, Eternal One, the holy God.

al hanisim by stacy beyer

for the miracles

hebrew: amidah (hoda'ah) & chanukah liturgy
music & english: stacy beyer

This song means so much to me, because it reflects the great energy and positive attitude that is so much a part of our faith. The vocal (a rock *niggun*), starts immediately on the first downbeat. The pace is fast and exciting as the band pushes ahead until the solo, where an expressive mandolin helps to quiet things down, only to build momentum again to the return of the *niggun*, which carries the song to its end. No words, just the joy of the *niggun* -- a celebration, carried on the wings of the music.

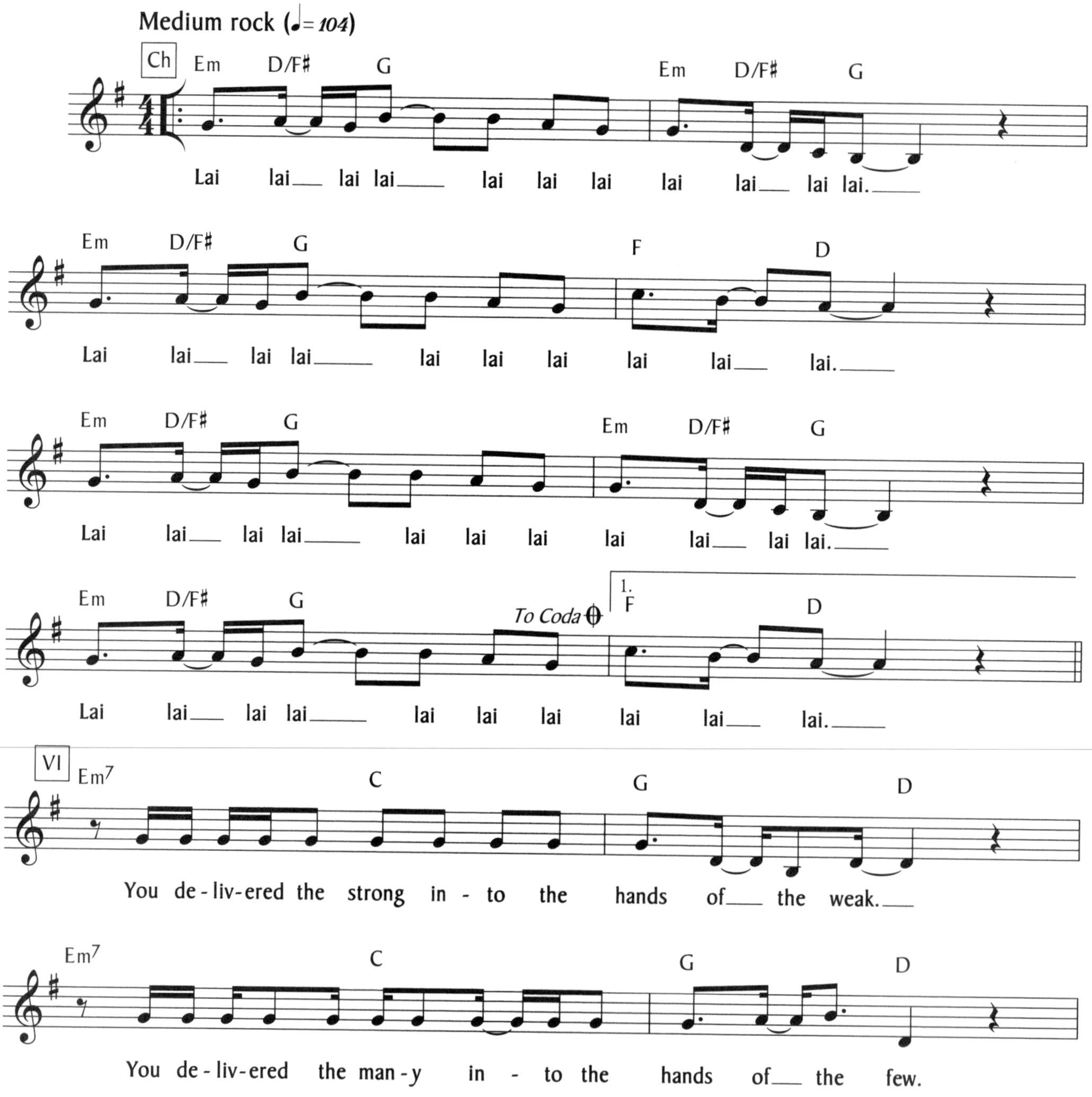

Medium rock (♩= 104)

Ch

Em D/F# G Em D/F# G
Lai lai___ lai lai___ lai lai lai lai lai___ lai lai.___

Em D/F# G F D
Lai lai___ lai lai___ lai lai lai lai lai___ lai.___

Em D/F# G Em D/F# G
Lai lai___ lai lai___ lai lai lai lai lai___ lai lai.___

Em D/F# G *To Coda* 1. F D
Lai lai___ lai lai___ lai lai lai lai lai___ lai.___

VI

Em7 C G D
You de-liv-ered the strong in - to the hands of___ the weak.___

Em7 C G D
You de-liv-ered the man-y in - to the hands of___ the few.

Am7 Em7 F C D G
3
You de-liv ered the wick ed to the righ - teous ones.__ Judged their__ cause,__
C D Em F D
heard their__ plea,__ and showed Your a - bun - dant mer - cy.__
2.
F D
V2
Em7 C G D
lai lai__ lai.__ Al ha-nis-sim__ v' - al ha - pur-kan__
Em7 C G D
v' - al__ ha - g'vu-rot v' - al ha - t'shu - ot
Am7 Em7 F C D G
v'-al__ ha - mil - cha - mot she-a - si - ta__ la - a - vo - tei - nu
C D Em F D
ba - ya - mim__ ha - heim ba - z'man ha - zeh.
3.
F D
Br
Em7 C
lai lai__ lai.__ And af - ter this Your chil - dren
(Af - ter this)
G D Em7 C
en - tered__ the shrine. And af - ter this Your house was
(Af - ter this)

עַל הַנִּסִּים וְעַל הַפֻּרְקָן וְעַל הַגְּבוּרוֹת
וְעַל הַתְּשׁוּעוֹת וְעַל הַמִּלְחָמוֹת שֶׁעָשִׂיתָ
לַאֲבוֹתֵינוּ בַּיָּמִים הָהֵם בַּזְּמַן הַזֶּה.

[We are grateful] for the miracles, for the redemption, for heroic acts, for saving deeds, and for all the battles You waged for our ancestors long ago at this time of year.

v'ahavta by rick recht

love your neighbor

hebrew: pirkei avot
music & english: rick recht

I think one of the most inspiring and empowering aspects of Judaism is the notion that every individual is called on to make a positive difference in this world and that we should do so with a deep sense of appreciation for the blessings we've received. When I wrote "V'ahavta," I was thinking about all the blessings I have been given in my life and how I feel so incredibly lucky that I actually sort of shout it out loud inside my head, "You've got this life to live ... Live it!" It's my little bizarre personal way of reminding myself to get up every morning and jolt myself into making a difference in this world.

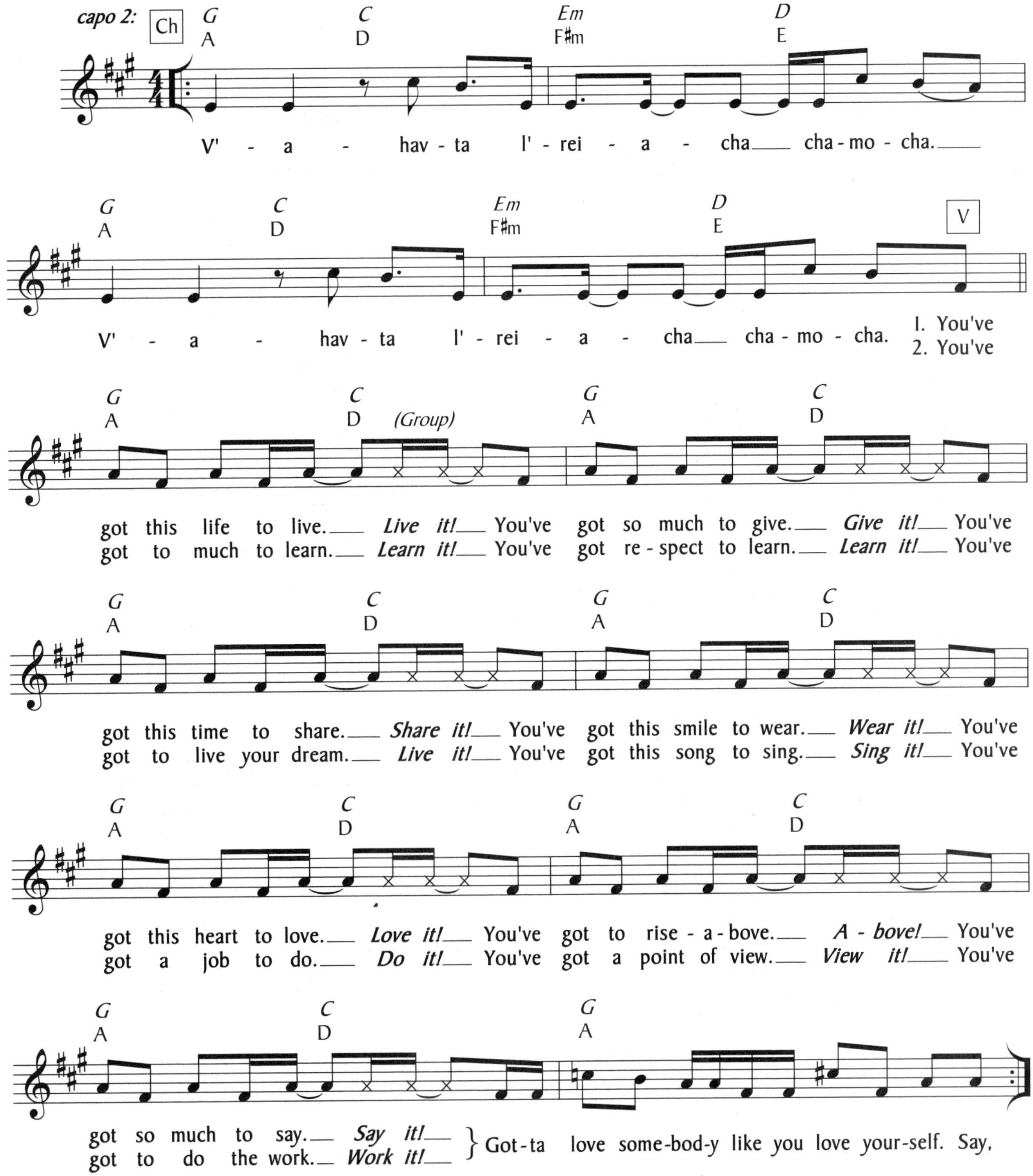

capo 2: Ch *G* A *C* D *Em* F♯m *D* E

V' - a - hav - ta l' - rei - a - cha cha - mo - cha.

G A *C* D *Em* F♯m *D* E V

V' - a - hav - ta l' - rei - a - cha cha - mo - cha. 1. You've 2. You've

G A *C* D *(Group)* *G* A *C* D

got this life to live. *Live it!* You've got so much to give. *Give it!* You've
got to much to learn. *Learn it!* You've got re - spect to learn. *Learn it!* You've

G A *C* D *G* A *C* D

got this time to share. *Share it!* You've got this smile to wear. *Wear it!* You've
got to live your dream. *Live it!* You've got this song to sing. *Sing it!* You've

G A *C* D *G* A *C* D

got this heart to love. *Love it!* You've got to rise - a - bove. *A - bove!* You've
got a job to do. *Do it!* You've got a point of view. *View it!* You've

G A *C* D *G* A

got so much to say. *Say it!* } Got - ta love some - bod - y like you love your - self. Say,
got to do the work. *Work it!* }

וְאָהַבְתָּ לְרֵעֲךָ, לְרֵעֲךָ כָּמוֹךָ *You shall love your neighbor as yourself.*

yih'yu l'ratzon by the josh nelson project

may the words

text: amidah (birkat shalom)
music: josh nelson

> Nothing defines us more than our thoughts and our words. We laugh, we argue, we shout, we dream ... and we paint pictures of who we really are. Every word is a chance to uplift another person, and every thought is an opportunity to remember the teachings that guide us. Life is short. Make it count.

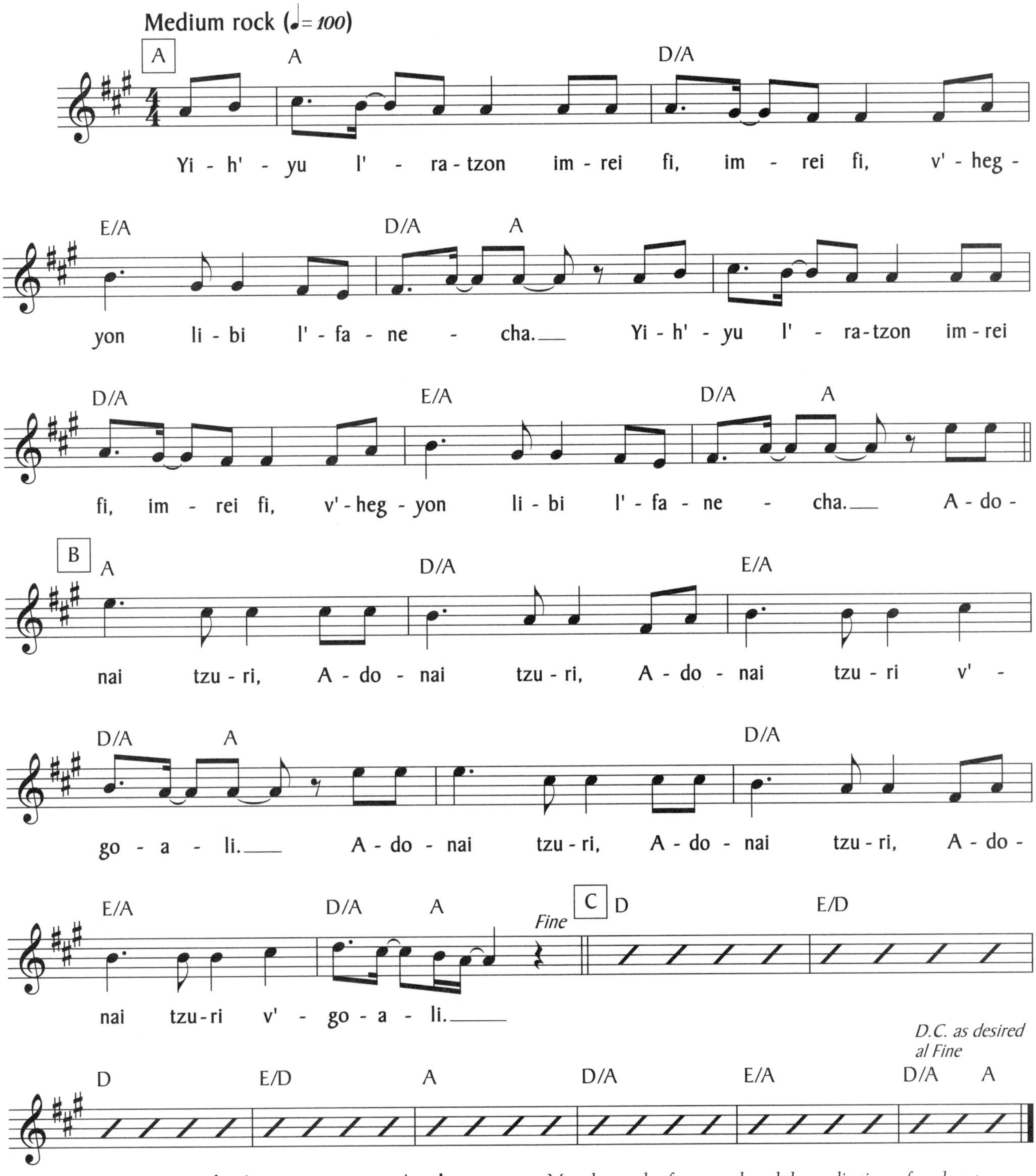

Medium rock (♩= *100*)

A

A D/A
Yi - h' - yu l' - ra - tzon im - rei fi, im - rei fi, v' - heg -

E/A D/A A
yon li - bi l' - fa - ne - cha.___ Yi - h' - yu l' - ra - tzon im - rei

D/A E/A D/A A
fi, im - rei fi, v' - heg - yon li - bi l' - fa - ne - cha.___ A - do -

B

A D/A E/A
nai tzu - ri, A - do - nai tzu - ri, A - do - nai tzu - ri v' -

D/A A D/A
go - a - li.___ A - do - nai tzu - ri, A - do - nai tzu - ri, A - do -

E/A D/A A *Fine*
nai tzu - ri v' - go - a - li.___

C

D E/D

D E/D A D/A E/A D/A A

D.C. as desired al Fine

יִהְיוּ לְרָצוֹן אִמְרֵי־פִי וְהֶגְיוֹן לִבִּי
לְפָנֶיךָ, יְיָ, צוּרִי וְגוֹאֲלִי.

May the words of my mouth and the meditations of my heart be acceptable to You, God, my Rock and my Redeemer.

sow in tears, reap in joy

by debbie friedman

words & music: debbie friedman

The poets and sages of ancient times knew that the experience of being overwhelmed and overcome with feelings was not something from which one could escape. Their thinking was that in moments when we are overcome and feeling the depths of our pain, we need to take a break and think again. If we have the capacity to feel deep pain, we have the capacity to experience joy in the same proportion.

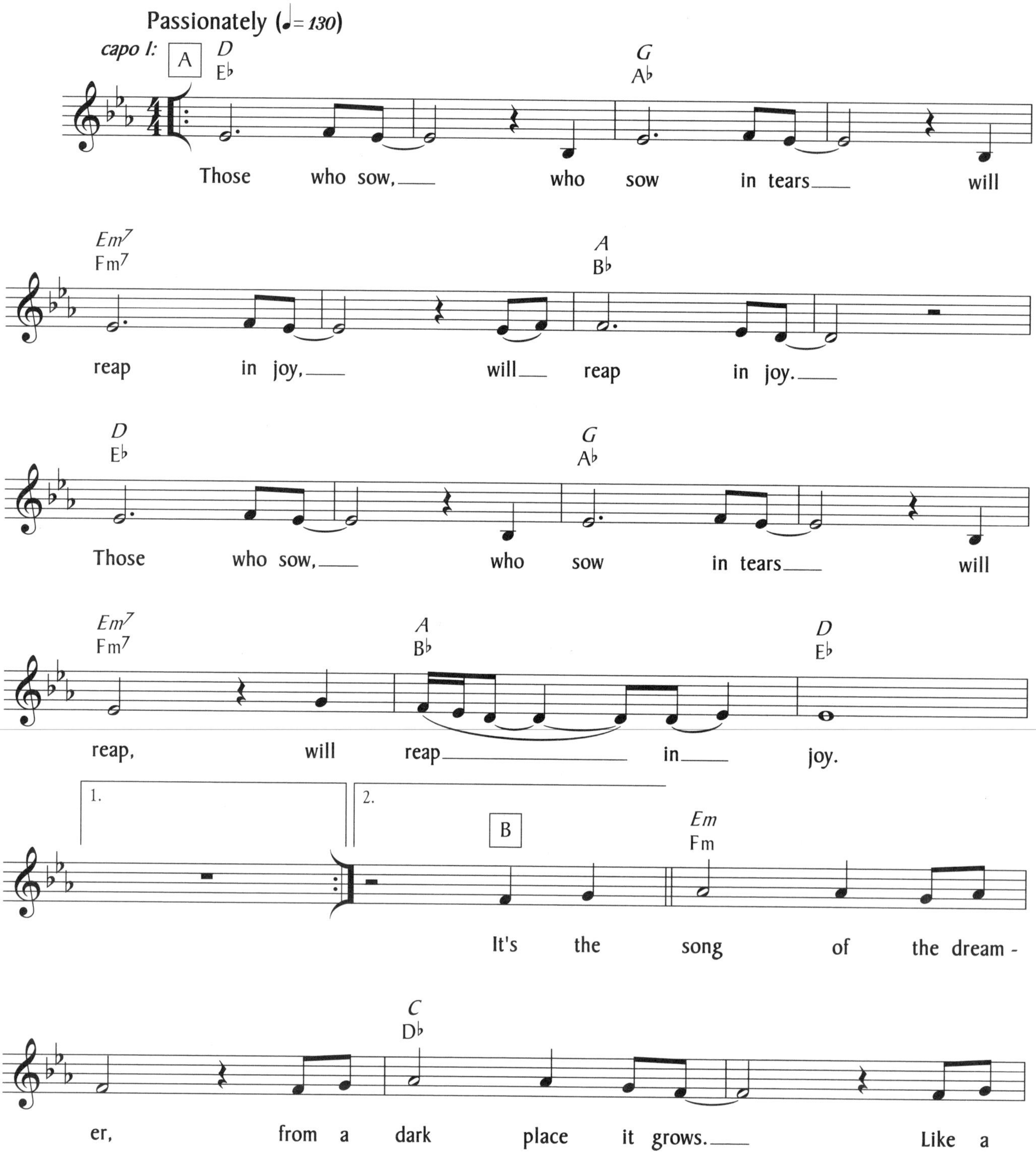

Passionately (♩= 130)

capo I: A D E♭ G A♭

Those who sow, who sow in tears will

Em7 Fm7 A B♭

reap in joy, will reap in joy.

D E♭ G A♭

Those who sow, who sow in tears will

Em7 Fm7 A B♭ D E♭

reap, will reap in joy.

1. 2. B Em Fm

It's the song of the dream-

C D♭

er, from a dark place it grows. Like a

G
A♭
D
E♭
flower in the des - ert, the o - a - sis of our souls.
Em
Fm
Come back, come back where we be-long,
A7
B♭7
C
D♭
you who hear our long-ing cries. Our mouths, our lips are
A
B♭
D.C. 2x, then repeat A section as desired
filled with song. You can see our tear - filled eyes.

modeh ani by noam katz

i give thanks

text: morning liturgy
music: noam katz and mike mason

Mike Mason and I wrote this on the porch of our T.C. cabins at Kutz Camp in the summer of 2002. Having been raised on the harmonies of Kol B'seder, we were excited to try a fresh take on this text, words of gratitude that one recites upon waking up in the morning. As much as we enjoyed our sleep that summer, we arose to the opportunities and challenges of each new day, giving thanks to God for reviving our souls and restoring our much-needed energy.

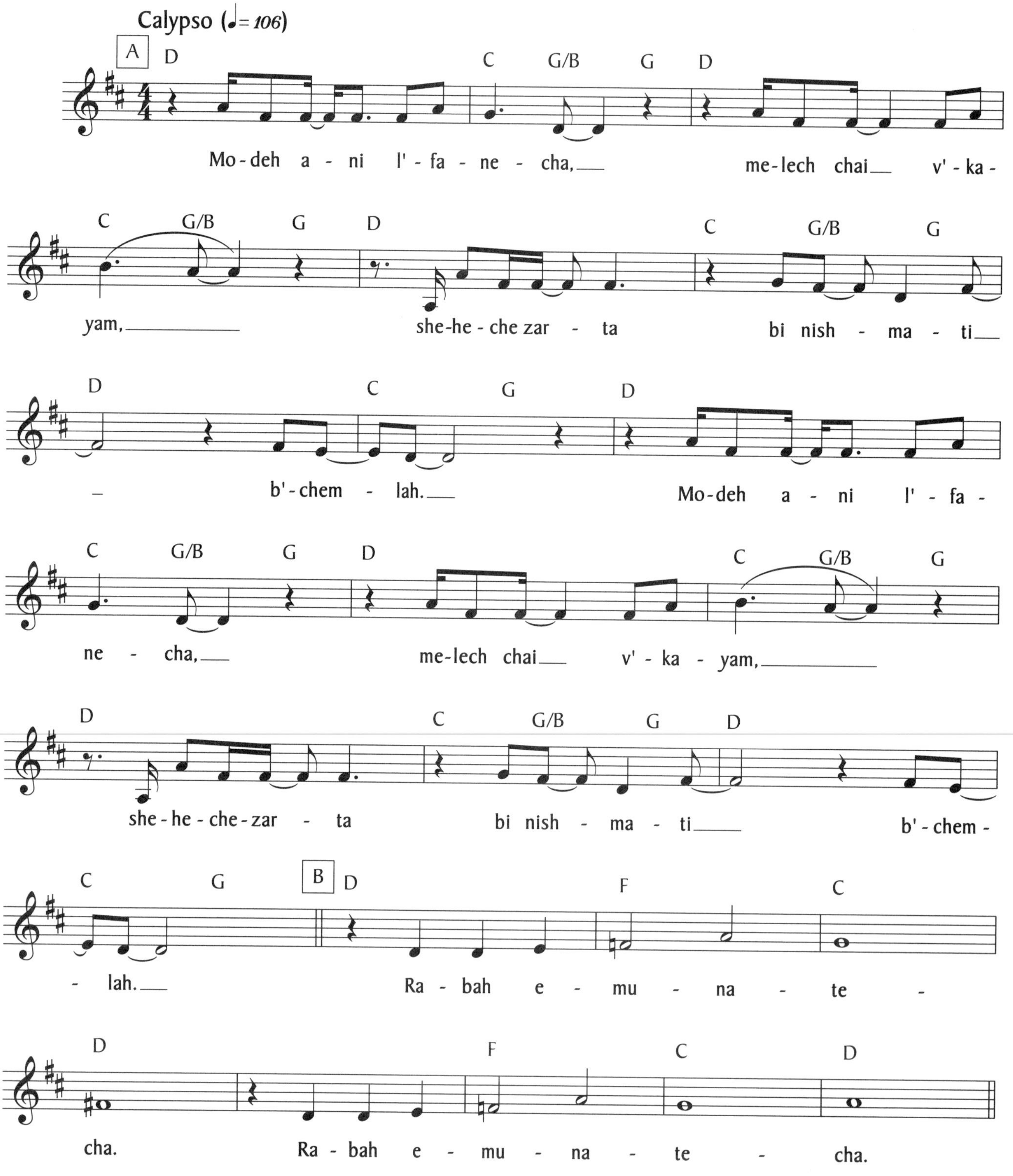

Calypso (♩= 106)

A

D C G/B G D

Mo-deh a - ni l' - fa - ne - cha, me-lech chai v' - ka -

C G/B G D C G/B G

yam, she-he - che zar - ta bi nish - ma - ti

D C G D

– b' - chem - lah. Mo-deh a - ni l' - fa -

C G/B G D C G/B G

ne - cha, me-lech chai v' - ka - yam,

D C G/B G D

she - he - che - zar - ta bi nish - ma - ti b' - chem -

C G B D F C

- lah. Ra - bah e - mu - na - te -

D F C D

cha. Ra - bah e - mu - na - te - cha.

C
Reggae
A G A
I give thanks to You, for You a - wak -
G A G
- en my soul. And I'll sing my praise to you,
A G
1.
D Calypso
for You have faith in me,
C G D C G
You have faith in me.
D C G D C G
D
2.
D9 Funk
me, You have faith in me.
Mo-deh a-ni l' - fa - ne - cha, me-lech chai v' - ka - yam,
she-he-che zar - ta bi nish - ma - ti b' chem - lah,
b' chem - lah. Ra - bah e - mu - na - te - cha.

מוֹדֶה אֲנִי לְפָנֶיךָ, מֶלֶךְ חַי
וְקַיָּם שֶׁהֶחֱזַרְתָּ בִּי נִשְׁמָתִי
בְּחֶמְלָה, רַבָּה אֱמוּנָתֶךָ.

I give thanks to You, O everlasting Ruler, for You have returned my soul to me in mercy. Great is Your faithfulness.

home by six13

words & music: alan zeitlin & mike boxer
choral arrangement: mike boxer

It's telling to see how images from Israel are presented. After a suicide bomber detonated himself aboard a bus and killed several passengers, the bus driver was interviewed from his hospital bed. When asked what he was going to do now, he said, calmly, that he would drive another bus. Asked why he wouldn't pick up and leave Israel out of fear, after narrowly avoiding death, he paused and said simply: "This is my home." This song is written from his perspective.

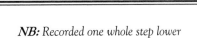

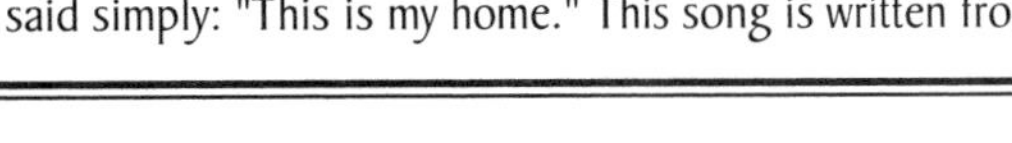

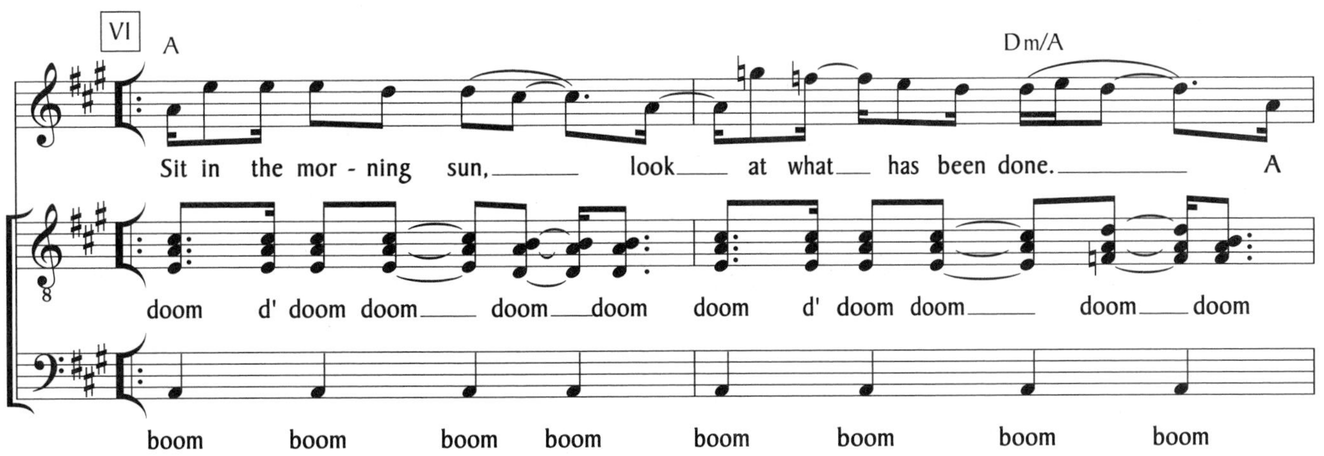

A
B♭
spin ning wheel in my hands, too late when we see the e - vil plans.
doom d' doom doom doom doom doom d' doom doom doom doom
boom boom boom boom boom boom boom boom
A
Dm/A
Eyes in-spect all who look strange, is that tired or is he de-ranged?
doom d' doom doom doom doom doom d' doom doom doom doom
boom boom boom boom boom boom boom boom
A
Chl
Trav-el-ers re - ly on me to get from point A to B. This is my
doom d' doom doom doom doom doom d' doom doom
boom boom boom boom boom boom
B♭
B♭add9
F
home, this is my moth - er - land. This is the place
Ja na jt dt dt ja na na jt dt dt ja na na jt dt dt ja na na jt dt dt ja
Doo doot doo doo doo doot doo doo doo doot doo doo doo doot doo doo

B♭
A
Dm
where I want to be, a home no one can take a - way from me. This is my
na na jt dt dt ja na na jt dt dt ja na na jt dt dt ja na na. Ja
doo doot doo doo doo doot doo doo doo doot doo doo doot my
B♭
B♭add9
F
3
home, this is my moth - er - land. This is the land
na na jt dt dt ja na na jt dt dt ja na na jt dt dt ja na na jt dt dt ja
doo doot doom doom doom doom doo doo doot doo doo doo doot doo doo
B♭
A
Dm
of streets paved with gold, this is the land of which my fath - ers told. This is my
na na jt dt dt ja na na jt dt dt ja na na jt dt dt ja na na. Ja
doo doot doo doo doo doot doo doo doo doot doo doo doot my
1.
B♭
A
Dm/A
home.
home. Doom d' doom doom doom doom doom d' doom doom doom doom
home.

See last page for Verse 2
& Chorus 2 lyrics
A
Dm/A
doom d' doom doom doom doom doom d' doom doom doom doom
Woom
2.
Aadd9
Br
Dm
C/D
home. My brother's not a number to mark down on a page. And
home. Ma ah
home. Ma da da dat da dat da dat da dat da dat da da dat da dat da dat da dat da dat da da
B♭/D
C/D
while I sit here grap - pl-ing with un - re - lent - ing rage. A
dat da dat da dat da dat da dat da da dat da dat da dat da dat da dat da da
Dm
Cadd9/D
C/D
3
face may be for - got - ten but the sight that still re - mains is the
ah
dat da dat da dat da dat da dat da da dat da dat da dat da dat da dat da da

B♭add9/D
B♭/D
Dsus4
D
Final Ch
pain-ful cries and tears and fears and streets filled with blood - stains. This is my
dat da dat da dat da dat da dat da da dat da dat da dat dow.
C
Cadd9
G
home, this is my moth - er land. This is the place
Ja na jt dt dt ja na na jt dt dt ja na na jt dt dt ja na na jt dt dt ja
Doo doot doo doo doo doot doo doo doo doot doo doo doo doot doo doo
C
B
Em
where I want to be, a home no one can take a - way from me. This is my
na na jt dt dt ja na na jt dt dt ja na na jt dt dt ja na na. Ja
doo doot doo doo doo doot doo doo doo doot doo doo doot doo doo
C
Cadd9
G
home, this is my cho - sen land. This is the place
na na jt dt dt ja na na jt dt dt ja na na jt dt dt ja na na jt dt dt ja
doo doot doom doom doom doom doo doo doot doo doo doo doot doo doo

Cadd9
B
Em
_ I live_ to de-fend, hoping the fight_ some-day_ comes to_ an end. This is my
na na jt dt dt ja_ na na jt dt dt ja na na jt dt dt ja_ na na. Ja
doo doot doo doo doo doot doo doo doo doot doo_ doo doot doo doo
C
Cadd9
G
home, this is my prom-ised land._ This is the place_
na na jt dt dt ja_ na na jt dt dt ja prom-ised land._ jt dt dt ja
doo doot doo doo doo doot doo doo prom-ised land._
Cadd9
B
Em
_ where I_ want to be, a home no one_ can take_ a - way_ from me. This is my
na na jt dt dt ja_ na na jt dt dt ja na na jt dt dt ja_ na na. Ja
doo doot doo doo doo doot doo doo doo doot doo_ doo doot doo doo
C
Cadd9
G
home, this is my this is the place_
na na jt dt dt ja_ na na jt dt dt ja on - ly land. Jt dt dt ja
doo doot doo doo doo doot doo doo on - ly land. Doom

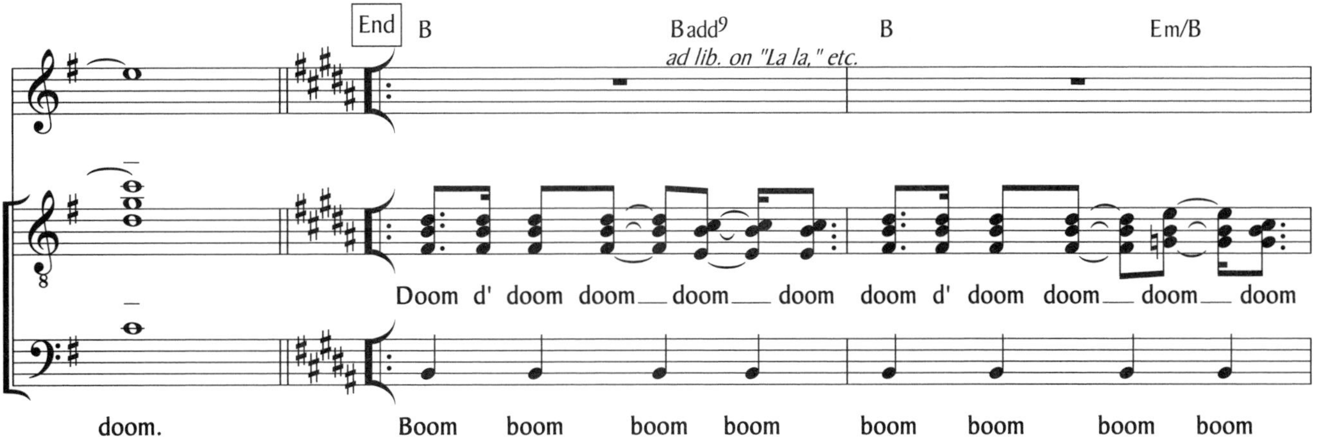

VERSE 2:
Here in my hospital bed,
  Wonder why it was not me instead.
Who knows who'll drop and who'll fall.
  Where's that voice that's supposed to call?
Is peace a sacred guest that's late?
  How best to digest what's on our plate?
There's a reason though we might not know;
  Forward's the only way to go.

CHORUS 2:
This is my home, this is my motherland.
This is the land that keeps us alive,
  This is the land for which my people strived.
This is my home, this is my motherland.
This is the place where I want to be,
  A home no one can take away from me.
This is my home. (To BRIDGE)

l'chu n'ran'nah by mah tovu

go forth singing

hebrew: psalms 95:1 & 96:1 **english:** ken chasen
music: ken chasen & josh zweiback

"L'chu N'ran'nah" is one of the psalms used to welcome Shabbat each week, so our goal with this setting was to express the joy of Shabbat … to celebrate God's wonder in our lives, and to give thanks for the marvels of creation. The English verses are designed to capture some of the poetry and key images of the Hebrew text. The music is designed to lift us up and move us to sing out to God with everything we've got.

Passionately (♩. = 50)

capo 5: Ch

Am Dm — G/A C/D — Am Dm — F B♭ — G C

L' - chu n' - ra - n' - nah... yai lai lai lai

Am Dm — G/A C/D — Am Dm — G/A C/D — Am Dm — F B♭ — G C

lai, la - do - nai... yai lai lai lai

Am Dm — G/A C/D — Am Dm — F B♭ — G C

lai, Na - ri - a... yai lai lai lai

Am Dm — G/A C/D — Am Dm — G/A C/D — Am Dm — F B♭ — G C — To Coda

lai, L' - tzur yish - ei - nu... yai lai lai lai

1 Am Dm — VI — F B♭ — G C

lai. Let us sing out to God, the Mak - er of all,

Em Am — F B♭ — Dm Gm

sure and strong. Let all of cre - a - tion from moun -

Em Am F B♭ E A E7 A7
- tain to sea hear our song. L' -
2 Am Dm V2 F B♭ G C
lai. For all of the won - der in all of God's light
Em Am F B♭ Dm Gm
we re - joice. So, now let us lis - ten with all
Em Am F B♭ E A E7 A7
of our hearts to hear God's voice. L' -
3 Am Dm Br B♭m E♭m
lai.
B♭m E♭m A♭/B♭ D♭/E♭ G♭ B A♭ D♭
Shi - ru, shi - ru shir la-do nai shi - ru shir cha -
1.2. B♭m E♭m A♭/B♭ D♭/E♭ 3. B♭m E♭m D.S. al Coda Gm Cm
dash. dash. L' - chu n' - ra - n' - nah, l' -
B♭m E♭m D♭m G♭m
chu n' - ra - n' - nah, l' - chu n' - ra - n' - nah.

לְכוּ נְרַנְּנָה לַייָ נָרִיעָה לְצוּר יִשְׁעֵנוּ.
שִׁירוּ לַייָ שִׁיר חָדָשׁ.

Go forth singing songs of joy to God. Let us shout joyfully to our Savior. Sing a new song to God.

one small step by peri smilow & the freedom music project

ruach 5767 track 10

text & music: peri smilow, based on midrash

When I learned the midrash about Nachshon and thought about the small but ultimately life-changing steps that he took into the waters of the Red Sea, I couldn't help but wonder about the power that each one of us has to take our own "small steps." Nachshon's faith, combined with action, led to the parting of the waters and to freedom for our people. I wrote this song with the hope that it might inspire more acts of faith in this broken world. Maybe all it will take to heal our world is for each one of us to take "One Small Step."

Hip-hop (♩= 80) (Swung 16th's)
Am F G E7 Am F G Am VI
Nach -
FMaj7 G Am
shon ben A - mi - na - dav was just one face in the crowd. He was
F G/F E7sus4 E7
tired and he was hun - gry, scared but he was proud. He had
Am FMaj7 G Am
walked a - cross the des-ert to es - cape sla - ve - ry and now he's
FMaj7 G/F E7sus4 E7
caught be-tween his task-mas-ters and the wa-ters of the Red Sea.
Am FMaj7 G Am
Phar - aoh and his ar - my were com-in' up fast from be-hind, and the
FMaj7 G E7
Is - rael-ites were ar - gu-ing, they were of two minds. Some

Am FMaj7 G Am
said, "We should turn a-round, go back to what we know.
FMaj7 E7sus4 E7
Sla - very can't be half as bad as drown - ing." You got-ta take
Ch Am FMaj7 G E7 Am FMaj7
One small step, one small step. You got-ta take one small step for
G Am Am FMaj7
free - - - dom. You got-ta take One small step,
G E7 Am FMaj7 To Coda G Am To Verses
one small step. You got-ta take one small step for free - dom. (2.) The
V2 Am FMaj7 G Am
oth-er side, well, they were ver-y few said, "No, this can-not be. We
F FMaj7 E7sus4 E7
can't go back, we've come so far in flee-ing sla - ve-ry. If you
Am FMaj7 G Am
just stay put, I think you'll find that God will make a move, and a
FMaj7 E7sus4 E7 D.S.
mir-a-cle will save us all — Just wait." You got-ta take

V3
Am
FMaj7
G
Am
No one no-ticed Nach-shon o-ver by the rip-pling tide. He had
FMaj7
E7sus4
E7
one foot in the wa-ter, his shoes at his side. He took
Am
Slowly and freely, with suspense
FMaj7
G
Am
one step, then an-oth-er 'til he could bare-ly breathe, and just
FMaj7
E7sus4
A tempo
E7
when the world went dark, the wa-ters part-ed and we were free.
D.S. al Coda
'Cause he took
CODA
G
Am
free - dom!

egypts to leave by mark aaron james

Believe it or not, I was commisioned to write this song by an Episcopal church in Nashville. They knew I was a Jewish songwriter and they needed a song for a Passover service. I tried to incoporate several takes on what Passover meant to everyone and why it was important to use the lessons from the past for our future. I wanted to address the literal as well as the metaphorical lessons in the Passover story. Metophorically, we all have our own Egypts to leave. I was really happy to get the four questions in there as well.

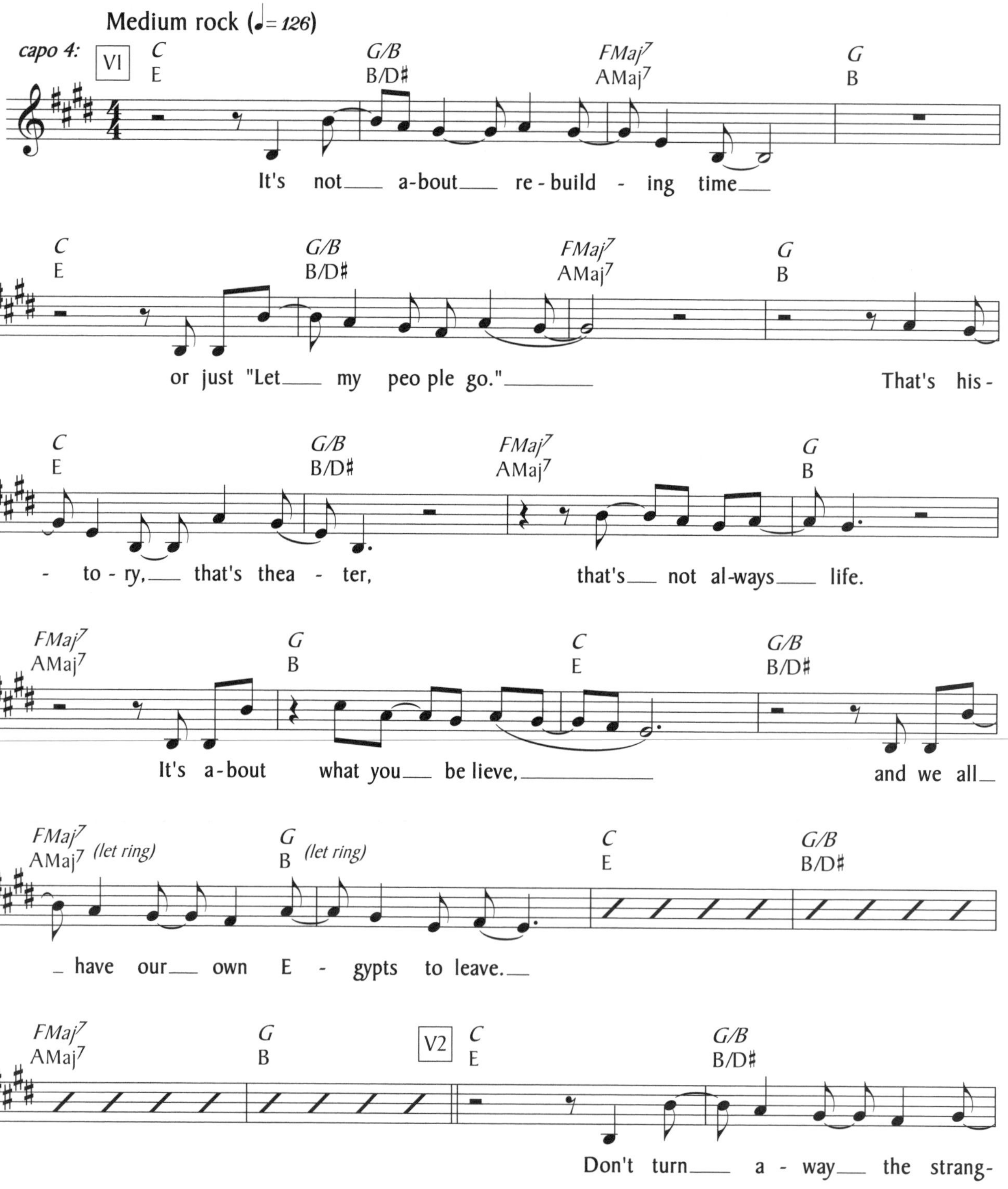

Medium rock (♩= 126)

capo 4: V1

It's not a-bout re-build-ing time
or just "Let my peo ple go."
That's his-to-ry, that's thea-ter,
that's not al-ways life.
It's a-bout what you be lieve,
and we all have our own E-gypts to leave.

V2

Don't turn a-way the strang-

FMaj7 AMaj7 G B C E G/B B/D♯
- er, for now you know the strang - er's heart
FMaj7 AMaj7 G B C E G/B B/D♯
from his - to - ry, from thea - ter,
FMaj7 AMaj7 G B FMaj7 AMaj7 G B
some times that's life. It comes down to what you be lieve,
C E G/B B/D♯ FMaj7 AMaj7 (let ring) G B (let ring)
and we all have our own E - gypts to leave.
Ch
FMaj7 AMaj7 G B C E
We look back in or - der to look for - ward. We see that
3
G/B B/D♯ FMaj7 AMaj7 G B
we are a - mong re-demp - tions and acts of free dom and
C E G/B B/D♯ FMaj7 AMaj7 G B
births of pos - si - bil - i - ty. We might not have seen,
C E FMaj7 AMaj7 F A (let ring) G B (let ring)
To Coda
we all have our own E - gypts to leave.

C E G/B B/D♯ FMaj7 AMaj7 G B
Yeah, yeah.
C E G/B B/D♯ FMaj7 AMaj7
Why's it this way? Why on this night? Why not that way? Why
G B C E G/B B/D♯ FMaj7 AMaj7
not up - right? 'Cause of what He did for me
G B FMaj7 AMaj7 G B C E
and to show Him we be lieve,
G/B B/D♯ FMaj7 AMaj7 (let ring) G B (let ring) D.S. 𝄋 al Coda 𝄌
and we all have our own E - gypts to leave.
𝄌 CODA
C E G/B B/D♯ FMaj7 AMaj7
Why's it this way? Why on this night? Why not that way? Why
G B FMaj7 AMaj7 (ad lib.) G B
not up - right? We look back in or - der to look for -

C E G/B B/D♯ FMaj7 AMaj7
3
- ward. We see that we are a-mong re-demp - tions and
G B C E G/B B/D♯
acts of free-dom and births of pos - si-bil - i - ty.
FMaj7 AMaj7 G B C E FMaj7 AMaj7
We might not have seen, we all
F A (let ring) G B (let ring) C E
have our own E - gypts to leave.
G/B B/D♯ FMaj7 AMaj7 G B C E
Yeah, yeah. E - gypts to leave.
G/B B/D♯ FMaj7 AMaj7 G B FMaj7 AMaj7
Yeah, yeah.

hashkiveinu by dan nichols

let us lie down

hebrew: evening liturgy
music & english: dan nichols

The lyrical content of this song is especially meaningful when you think about it in context: "From generation to generation ... we will praise Your name." This song in particular has really got a to-the-minute contemporary feel to it, and that resonates with the newest generations of Judaism. As with all music, the sound and the style changes drastically from era to era, but Dan Nichols and his peers are doing their part to ensure that the constant—the Jewish connection to God—remains very much alive. -- *Mike Boxer*

Sweetly (♩ = 85)

capo 4: Ch

Em G♯m — *C* E — *G* B — *D* F♯

Hash - ki - vei - nu, A - do - nai

Em G♯m — *C* E — *G* B — *D* F♯ — *Em* G♯m — *C* E

E - lo - hei - nu, l' - sha - lom, v' - ha'a - mi - dei - nu, Mal -

G B — *D* F♯ — *C* E — *D* F♯ — *G* B

kei - nu, l' - cha - yim.

To Verses

V1

Am C♯m — *Am/G* C♯m/B — *D* F♯

Spread the shel - ter of Your peace o - ver us.

Am C♯m — *Am/G* C♯m/B — *D* F♯

Guide us in wis - dom, com - pas - sion, and trust.

D.C.

V2

Am C♯m — *Am/G* C♯m/B — *D* F♯

Save us for the sake of Your name.

הַשְׁכִּיבֵנוּ, יְיָ אֱלֹהֵינוּ, לְשָׁלוֹם,
וְהַעֲמִידֵנוּ, מַלְכֵּנוּ, לְחַיִּים.

Grant, O Eternal God, that we may lie down in peace, and raise us up, O Sovereign, to life renewed.

love multiplies by beth schafer

text & music: beth schafer

Love is not a pie that gets divided among all who come into your life. Love is like a flame forever multiplying; no matter how many candles you need to light. The more people you love, the more love there is. So love should never divide a family or a community, but only brighten it. As I was getting ready to give birth to my second child, I wondered if I would have enough love in me to love her, as I did my first. What a wonderful realization to learn that not only do I have a limitless capacity to love, but if I do, so does everyone. This is the realization that will one day heal the world.

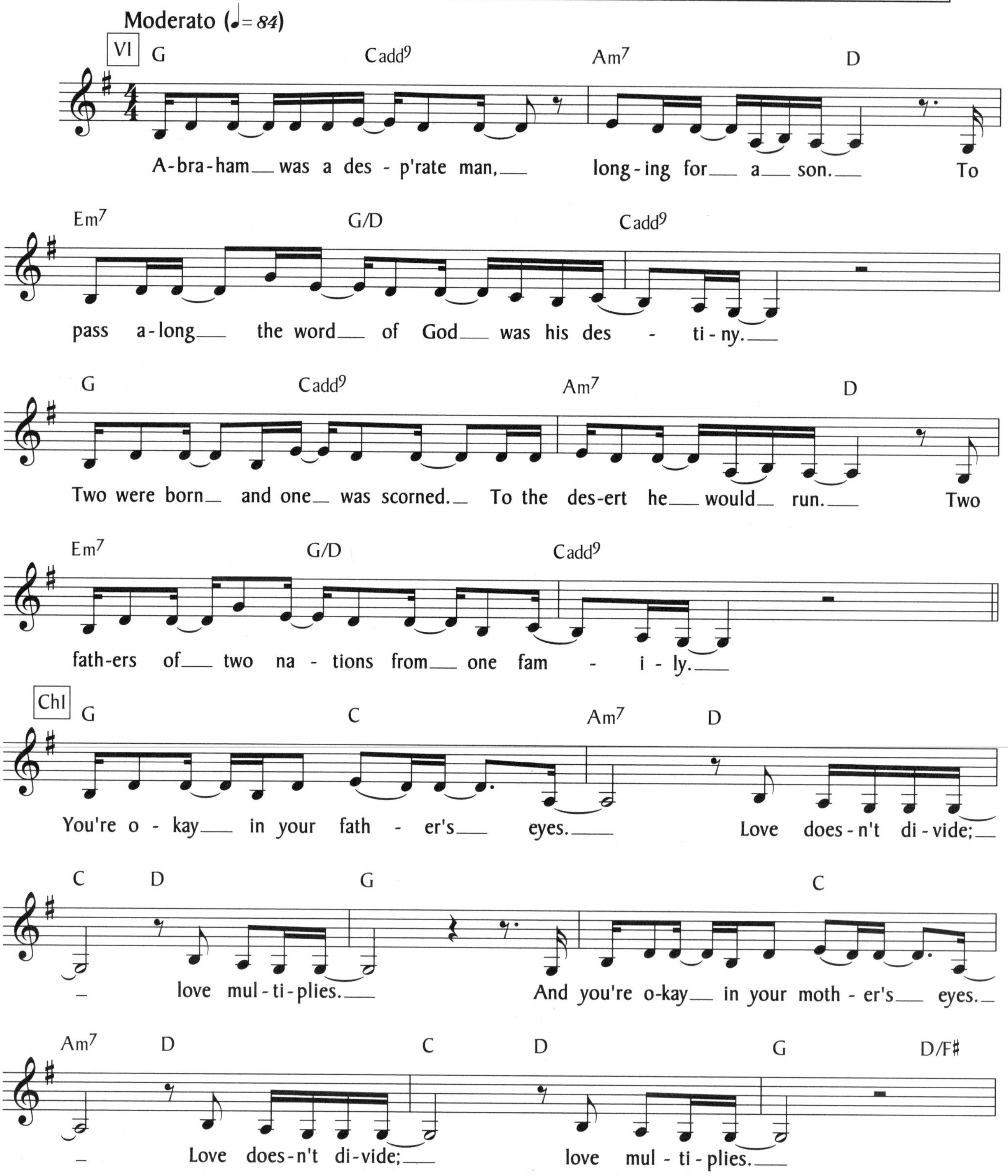

Moderato (♩= 84)

VI

G Cadd9 Am7 D

A-bra-ham__ was a des - p'rate man,__ long-ing for__ a__ son.__ To

Em7 G/D Cadd9

pass a-long__ the word__ of God__ was his des - ti - ny.__

G Cadd9 Am7 D

Two were born__ and one__ was scorned.__ To the des-ert he__ would__ run.__ Two

Em7 G/D Cadd9

fath-ers of__ two na - tions from__ one fam - i - ly.__

Chl

G C Am7 D

You're o - kay__ in your fath - er's__ eyes.__ Love does-n't di-vide;__

C D G C

– love mul-ti-plies.__ And you're o-kay__ in your moth - er's__ eyes.__

Am7 D C D G D/F♯

– Love does-n't di-vide;__ love mul - ti - plies.__

Em7 Bm7 Asus4 A
Fam-'lies fall and fam-'lies rise. Love does-n't di-vide;
C D G D/F♯ Em7 Bm7
love mul-ti-plies. Love your God and you'll be wise.
Asus4 A C D G
Love does-n't di-vide; love mul-ti-plies.
C G C
A
V2
G Cadd9 Am7 D
lit-tle town was bound to grow, des tined to be more. Ev-'ry
Em7 G/D Cadd9
year an-oth-er church would claim its place on the road. And each
G Cadd9 Am7 D
Sab bath day the folks would pray be-hind their bolt-ed doors, and the
Em7 G/D Cadd9
air would fill with notes of hope, on-ly who would know?
Ch2
G C Am7 D
You're o-kay in your neigh-bor's eyes. Love does-n't di-vide;

C D G C
love mul-ti-plies. And you're o-kay in the strang-er's eyes.
Am7 D C D G D/F♯
Love does-n't di-vide; love mul-ti-plies.
Em7 Bm7 Asus4 A
Ci-ties fall and ci-ties rise. Love does-n't di-vide;
C D G D/F♯ Em7 Bm7
love mul-ti-plies. Love your God and you'll be wise.
Asus4 A C D G
Love does-n't di-vide; love mul-ti-plies.
C G C
A
V3
G Cadd9 Am7 D
moth-er holds her lit-tle girl, who is the world to her, but she
Em7 G/D Cadd9
knows an-oth-er ba-by will be com-ing soon. This
G Cadd9 Am7 D
one on one lit-tle love af-fair will have to end for sure.

Em7 G/D Cadd9
How could her full heart come up with an - y more room?
Ch3
G C Am7 D
You're o - kay in your daugh - ter's eyes. Love does-n't di-vide;
C D G C
love mul-ti-plies. And you're o - kay in that ba - by's eyes.
Am7 D C D G D/F♯
Love does n't di-vide; love mul - ti-plies.
Em7 Bm7 Asus4 A
Keep on go - ing and claim - your prize. Love does-n't di-vide;
C D G D/F♯ Em7 Bm7
love mul - ti-plies. Love your God and you'll be
Asus4 A C
wise. Love does-n't di - vide;
D G C
love mul - ti-plies.
G C G
rit.

t'filat haderech/ never walk alone by ross m. levy

ruach 5767 track 14

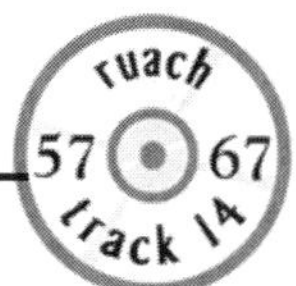

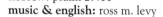

hebrew: psalm 29:11
music & english: ross m. levy

> My wife was going away for a few days to visit her family. She was busy packing and getting ready to leave for the airport. I was sitting on the floor in her room just kind of improvising a farewell to my beloved and "T'filat Haderech" was the result. It was one of those rare pieces that just came together naturally in only minutes.

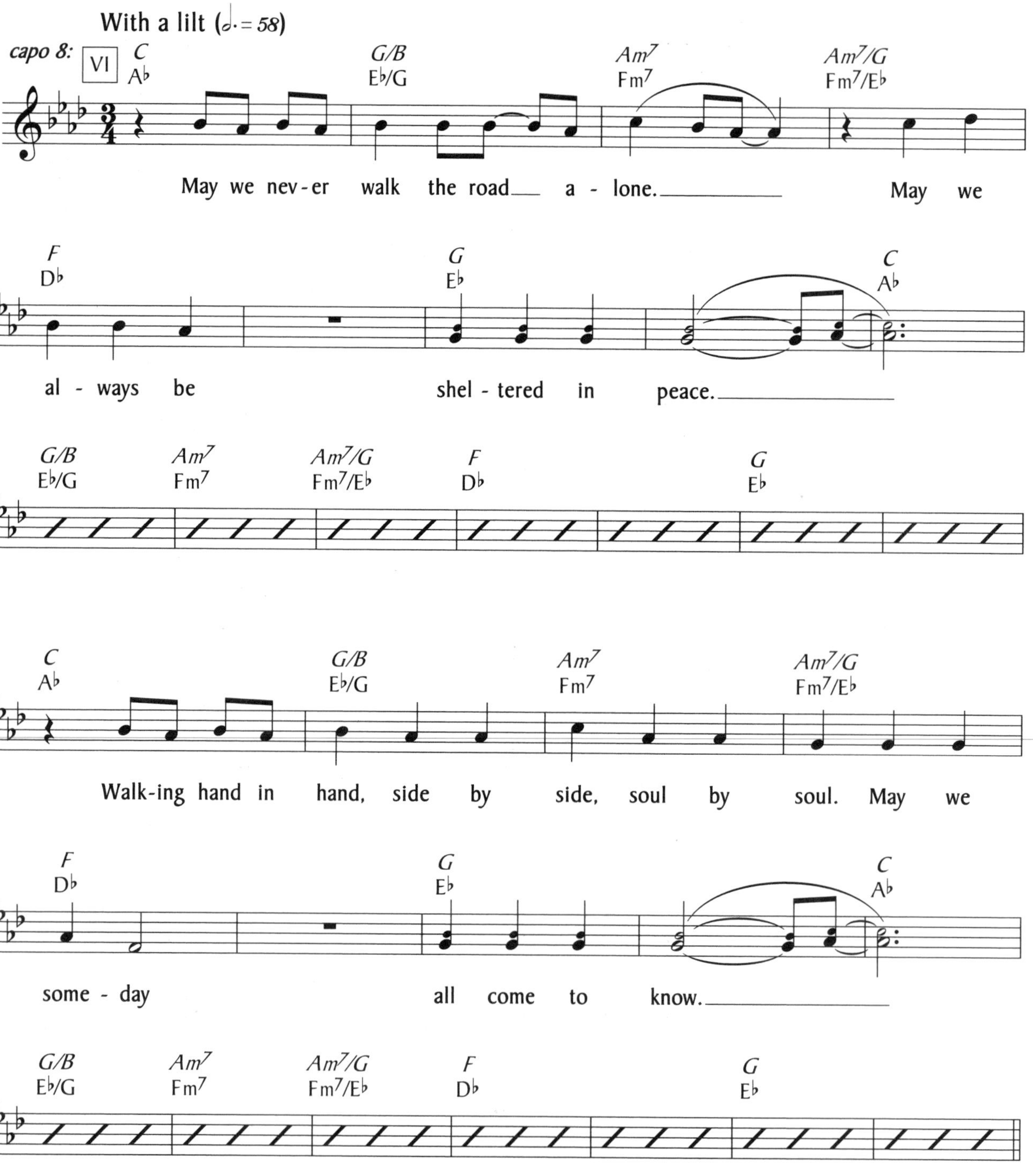

With a lilt (♩. = 58)
capo 8: VI
C Ab | G/B Eb/G | Am7 Fm7 | Am7/G Fm7/Eb
May we nev-er walk the road a - lone. May we
F Db | G Eb | C Ab
al - ways be shel - tered in peace.
G/B Eb/G | Am7 Fm7 | Am7/G Fm7/Eb | F Db | G Eb
C Ab | G/B Eb/G | Am7 Fm7 | Am7/G Fm7/Eb
Walk-ing hand in hand, side by side, soul by soul. May we
F Db | G Eb | C Ab
some - day all come to know.
G/B Eb/G | Am7 Fm7 | Am7/G Fm7/Eb | F Db | G Eb

Ch
C
A♭
G/B
E♭/G
Am7
Fm7
Am7/G
Fm7/E♭
May the ways of health and joy reach the hearts of each girl and
F
D♭
G
E♭
FMaj7
D♭Maj7
boy from now through for - ev - er,
Em7
Cm7
D
B♭
D/G
B♭/E♭
oh, from
D/F♯
B♭/D
FMaj7
D♭Maj7
Em7
Cm7
now through for - ev - er, oh.
D
B♭
D/G
B♭/E♭
D/F♯
B♭/D
V2
C
A♭
G/B
E♭/G
Am7
Fm7
Am7/G
Fm7/E♭
May we stroll the path that God has giv - en us. May we
F
D♭
G
E♭
C
A♭
al - ways be hap - py and free.
G/B
E♭/G
Am7
Fm7
Am7/G
Fm7/E♭
F
D♭

C G/B Am7 Am7/G
A♭ E♭/G Fm7 Fm7/E♭
Ev - 'ry step you take, take it safe - ly and in
F G C
D♭ E♭ A♭
ev - 'ry stride, find joy and pride.
G/B Am7 Am7/G F G
E♭/G Fm7 Fm7/E♭ D♭ E♭
C G/B Am7 Am7/G
A♭ E♭/G Fm7 Fm7/E♭
May we nev - er walk the road a - lone. May we
F G C
D♭ E♭ A♭
al - ways be shel - tered in peace.
G/B Am7 Am7/G F G
E♭/G Fm7 Fm7/E♭ D♭ E♭
Br
Am Em FMaj7
Fm Cm D♭Maj7
A - do - nai oz l' - a - mo yi - tein.
G Am Em
E♭ Fm Cm
A - do - nai oz l' - a -

יְיָ עֹז לְעַמּוֹ יִתֵּן.
יְיָ יְבָרֵךְ אֶת־עַמּוֹ בַשָּׁלוֹם.

May God give strength to our people.
May God bless our people with peace.

bayom hahu by steve dropkin

on that day

hebrew: liturgy
music & english: steve dropkin

Bayom Hahu was written as a way to praise God in a style that would be appealing to teenagers. The beat was an essential part of the song and the "twist of the English words" was intentional to show God true Oneness. I hope everyone enjoys this song!

Driving rock (♩= 148)

capo 5:* A

* *Capo top 5 strings only; 6th string remains open*

D/E Cadd9/Dadd9 G/A Cadd9/Dadd9 D/E

Yai dai dai yai dai dai dai dai, yai dai dai dai dai, yai dai dai dai dai dai.

Cadd9/Dadd9 G/A Cadd9/Dadd9 D/E

Yai dai dai yai dai dai dai dai, yai dai dai dai dai dai dai dai.

1. (repeat)

2. *Fine*

B D/E Cadd9/Dadd9 G/A Cadd9/Dadd9 D/E

Ba - yom ha - hu yi - h' - yeh A - do - nai, A - do - nai E - chad u - sh' - mo E - chad.

Cadd9/Dadd9 G/A Cadd9/Dadd9 D/E

Ba - yom ha - hu yi - h' - yeh A - do - nai, yi - h' - yeh A - do - nai E - chad. Now

בַּיּוֹם הַהוּא יִהְיֶה יְיָ
אֶחָד וּשְׁמוֹ אֶחָד.

On that day, God shall be One
and God's name shall be One.

bayom hahu by steve dropkin

on that day

hebrew: liturgy
music & english: steve dropkin

Bayom Hahu was written as a way to praise God in a style that would be appealing to teenagers. The beat was an essential part of the song and the "twist of the English words" was intentional to show God's true Oneness. I hope everyone enjoys this song!

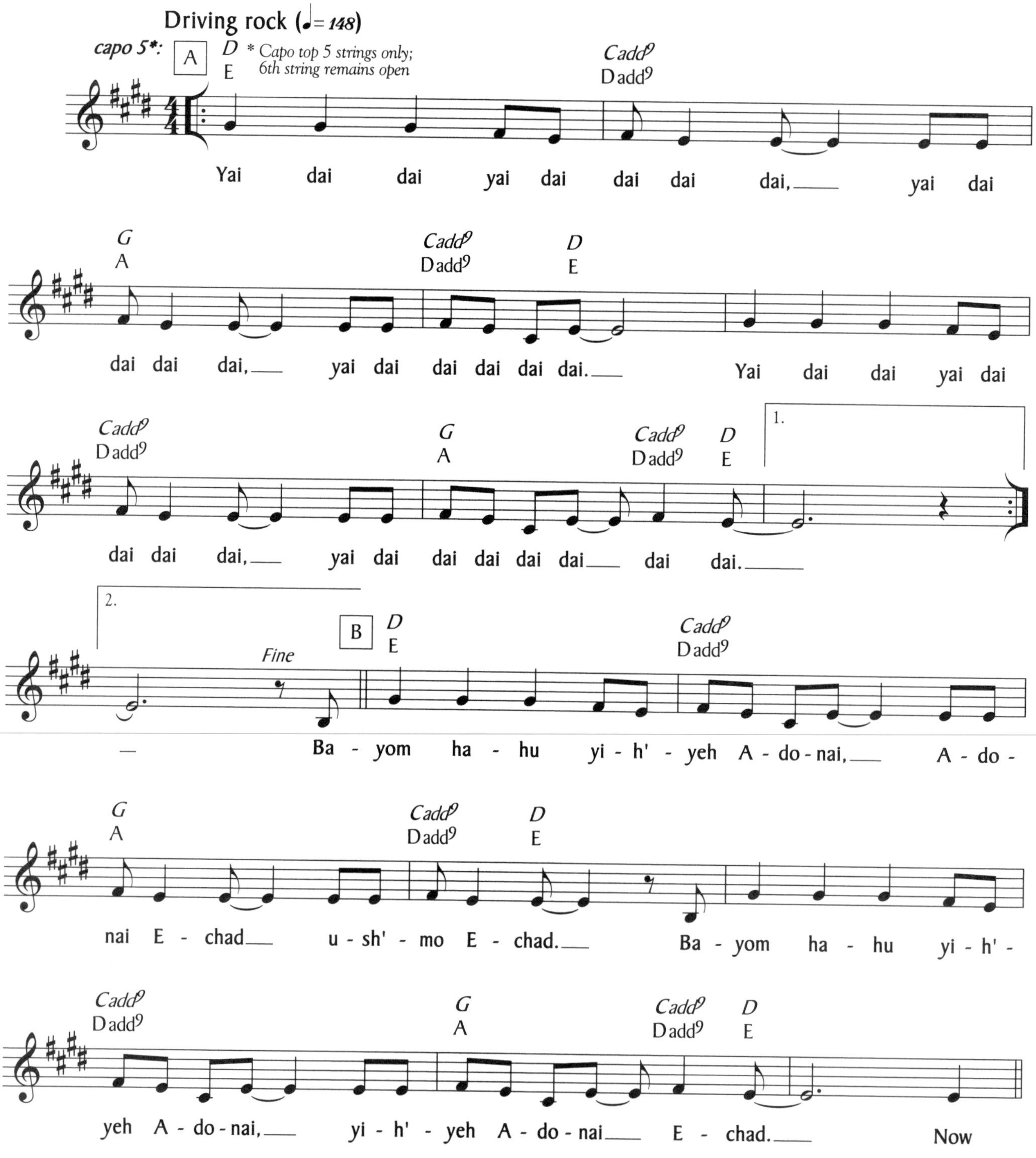

Driving rock (♩= 148)

capo 5*: A D E * Capo top 5 strings only; 6th string remains open

Cadd9 Dadd9

Yai dai dai yai dai dai dai dai, yai dai

G A Cadd9 Dadd9 D E

dai dai dai, yai dai dai dai dai dai. Yai dai dai yai dai

Cadd9 Dadd9 G A Cadd9 Dadd9 D E 1.

dai dai dai, yai dai dai dai dai dai dai dai.

2. Fine B D E Cadd9 Dadd9

Ba - yom ha - hu yi - h' - yeh A - do - nai, A - do -

G A Cadd9 Dadd9 D E

nai E - chad u - sh' - mo E - chad. Ba - yom ha - hu yi - h' -

Cadd9 Dadd9 G A Cadd9 Dadd9 D E

yeh A - do - nai, yi - h' - yeh A - do - nai E - chad. Now

בַּיּוֹם הַהוּא יִהְיֶה יְיָ
אֶחָד וּשְׁמוֹ אֶחָד.

On that day, God shall be One
and God's name shall be One.

ayzehu chacham by the josh nelson project

who is wise?

hebrew: pirkei avot 4:1
music & english: josh nelson

> Sometimes it's easy to stay in our comfort zone, to surround ourselves with people who feel, act, and believe as we do. Truth: The easy choice and the right choice are often different things. We will always be wiser when we listen with open minds to the words of those outside our circle. A better, stronger world is only built on a foundation of listening, understanding, and hope.

Rock (♩= 120)

D Dadd9/F♯ Gadd9

VI D Dadd9/F♯ Gadd9
Do you hear__ or do you lis - ten?

D Dadd9/F♯ Gadd9
Do you look__ or do__ you____ see?__

Bm7 Dadd9/A Gadd9
Can you feel__ a sep - a - ra - tion, be-cause of you,__

D Dadd9/F♯ Gadd9
– be-cause________ of me?__

D Dadd9/F♯ Gadd9
There are truths__ in one__ an - oth - er.

D Dadd9/F♯ Gadd9
There are trou - bles we__ have____ seen.__

Bm7 Dadd9/A Gadd9 D/F#
There is hope in un - der stan - ding.
Em7 Dadd9/F# Gadd9
There is life in the space be - tween.
Ch D Dadd9/F# Gadd9
Ay - ze - hu cha - cham? Ha - lo - meid,
D Dadd9/F# Gadd9
ha - lo - meid mi - kol a - dam.
D Dadd9/F# Gadd9
Ay - ze - hu cha - cham? Ha - lo - meid,
D Dadd9/F# Gadd9
ha - lo - meid mi - kol a - dam.
To Coda
1.
D Dadd9/F# Gadd9
V2
D Dadd9/F# Gadd9
Are we caught up in be - gin - nings,
D Dadd9/F# Gadd9
Speak ing first and hear - ing last?

Bm7
Dadd9/A
Gadd9
D/F♯
With all the les - sons we are learn - ing,
Em7
Dadd9/F♯
Gadd9
there's more to life than this bro - ken past.
Br
2.
F♯m7
Bm7
Can you make your cir - cle wid - er? Can you hear
Cadd9
what's there in - side her? Can you feel what's there be -
Gadd9
F♯m7
yond your door? Words that help
Bm7
you start to hear her, words that make the mes - sage clear -
Cadd9
er, words of bles - sing that we all are
CODA
D.S. 𝄋 al Coda
here for.
Gadd9
Dadd9

אִיזֶהוּ חָכָם? הַלּוֹמֵד מִכָּל אָדָם. *Who is wise? Those who learn from all people.*

hallel l'adonai b'chayai

by **the israeli mechina's *zimrat yah***

i will sing to god

words & music: annabel esperanta & noah ben gur, based on psalm 146:2

A capella, with percussion (♩= *88*)

Solo: A

A-ha - lei - lah A - do - nai___ b' - cha-yai, b' - cha - yai.

A - zam-rah lei - lo - hai b' - o - di, o-

divisi

Harmony: B

A-ha - lei - lah A - do - nai___ b' - cha - yai,

Melody:

di. A-ha - lei - lah A - do - nai___ b' - cha - yai,

b' - cha - yai. A - zam - rah lei - lo - hai

b' - cha - yai. A - zam - rah lei - lo - hai___

b' - o - di, o - di. A - ha -

b' - o - di, o - di. A - ha -

C
lei - lah A - do - nai b' - cha - yai, b' - cha - yai.
lei - lah A - do - nai b' - cha - yai, b' - cha - yai.
A - zam - rah lei - lo - hai b' - o -
A - zam - rah lei - lo - hai b' - o -
1.
2.
To Coda
di, o - di. A - ha - di.
di, o - di. A - ha - di.
D
Solo:
Solo:
Sha - mor sha - ma - ti kol A - do - nai kol A - do - nai
Tutti
Sha - mor sha - ma - ti kol A - do - nai,
D.S. al Coda
kol A - do - nai ho - shi - ah nah ho - shi - ah nah A - ha-
Tutti
kol A - do - nai ho - shi - ah nah ho - shi - ah - nah A - ha-

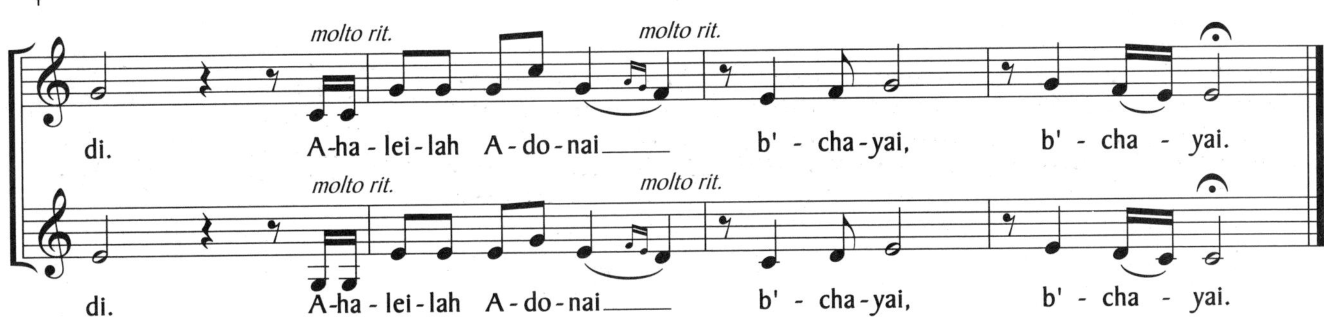

אֲהַלְלָה יְהוָה בְּחַיָּי
אֲזַמְּרָה לֵאלֹהַי בְּעוֹדִי:

I will praise God all my life, sing to my God with all my being!

hatikvah — don't give up the hope

by **eric komar**

music: based on *hatikvah* (the hope), arr. eric komar

This instrumental version of the Israeli national anthem was conceived in 1993, after I saw a photo of Yitzhak Rabin (z"l) and Yasser Arafat shaking hands at the Oslo Accords, with Bill Clinton standing behind them. Years after this historic event, we are still hoping to be truly free. This arrangement is in the style of jazz guitarist Joe Pass, whose solo virtuoso playing I can only aspire to emulate, but could never match!

Slightly faster
B
Bm11
A11
DMaj7
mp
Slightly slower = c. 104
C♯m11
CMaj7♭5
F°
A11
rit.
DMaj7♯5
F♯7♯9
Bm
Bm/A
Em
Bm
Bm/A
rit.
Em7
F♯7♭9
p
Animato (= c. 136)
Bm
Bm/A
G♯m7♭5
G7♭5
molto rit.
F♯7
F♯7♯5
C
Bm7
C♯m7

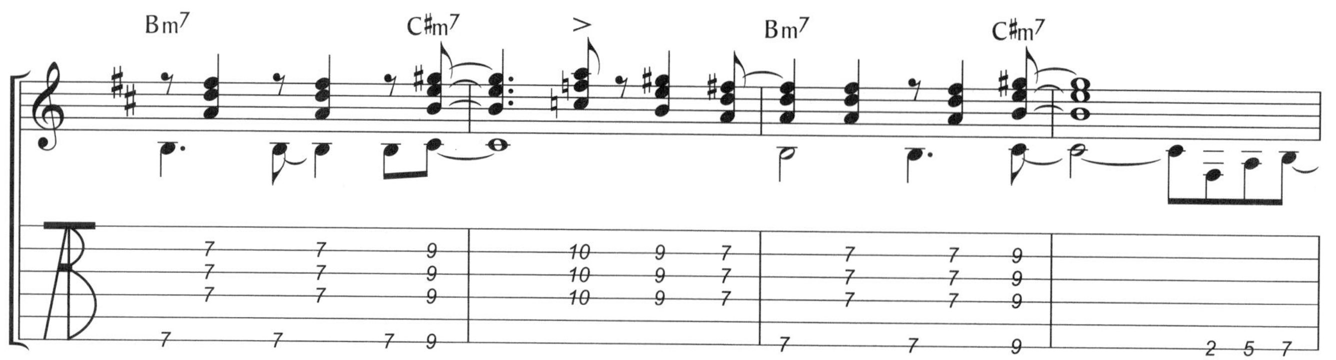
Bm7
C♯m7
Bm7
C♯m7

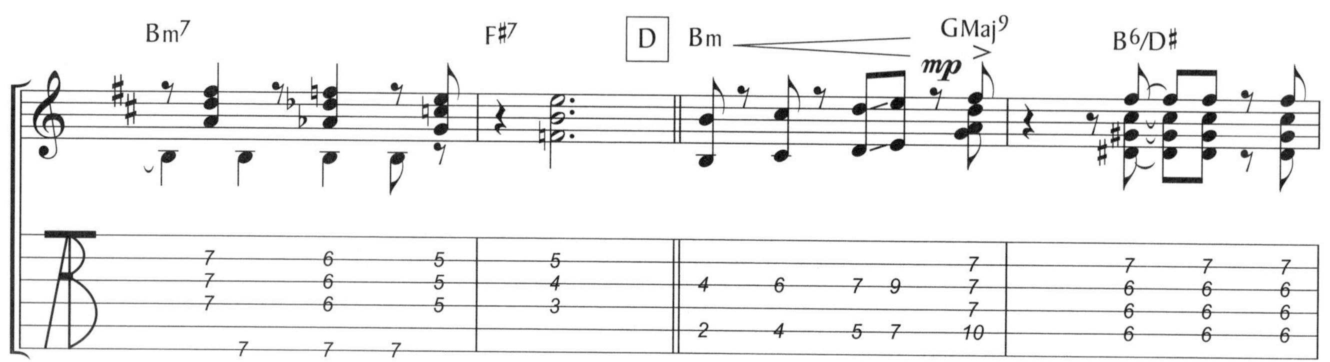
Bm7
F♯7
D
Bm
GMaj9
mp
B6/D♯

Em11
DMaj7
Am7
A♭m7♯5
Gm7
C9

Em6
F♯7♯5
Bm7
F♯7♯9♯5
F♯7♭9♯5
Bm7
F♯m9
F7♯9

Em11 B♭13 A13 Bm7
mf
C♯m7♭5 F♯7♯9♯5 F♯7♭9♯5 Bm7 G♯m7♭5
poco cresc.

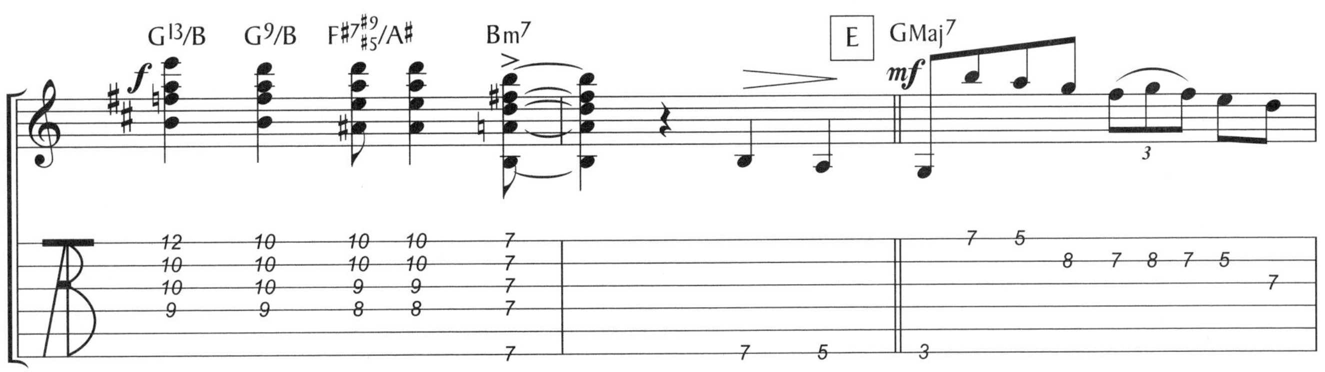
G13/B G9/B F♯7♯9♯5/A♯ Bm7
f
E
GMaj7
mf

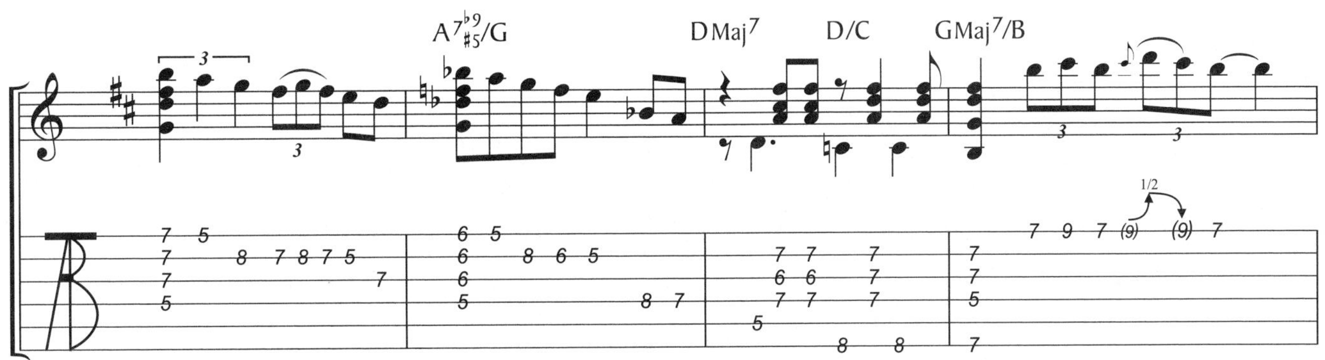
A7♭9♯5/G DMaj7 D/C GMaj7/B
1/2

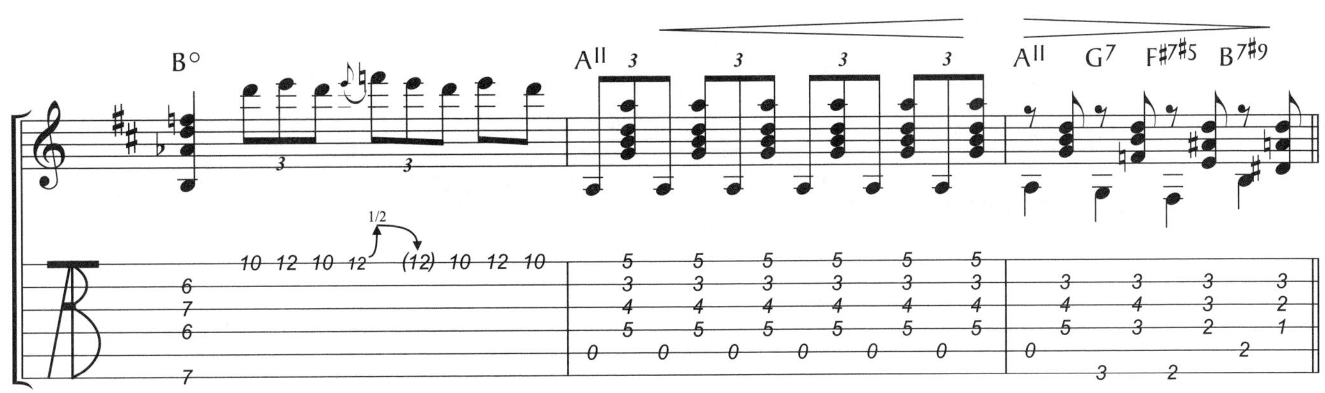
B°
1/2
A11
A11 G7 F♯7♯5 B7♯9

F
Em7
mf
Am7

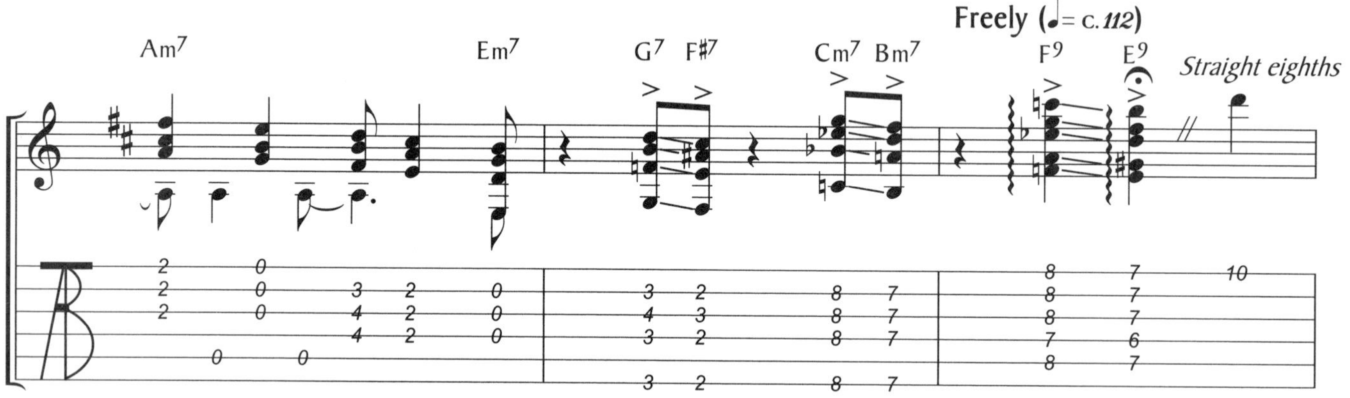
Am7
Em7
Freely (♩= c.112)
G7 F♯7
Cm7 Bm7
F9
E9
Straight eighths

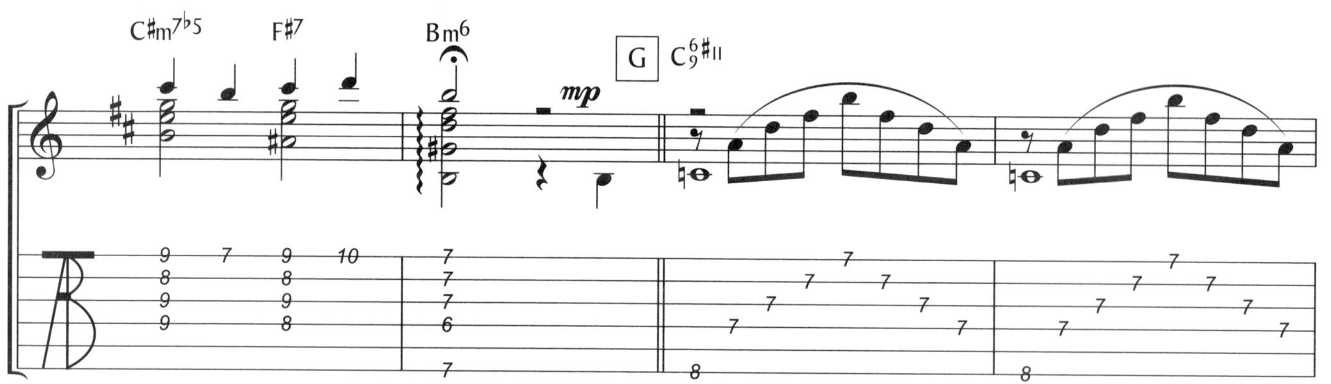
C♯m7♭5
F♯7
Bm6
mp
G
C6 9♯11

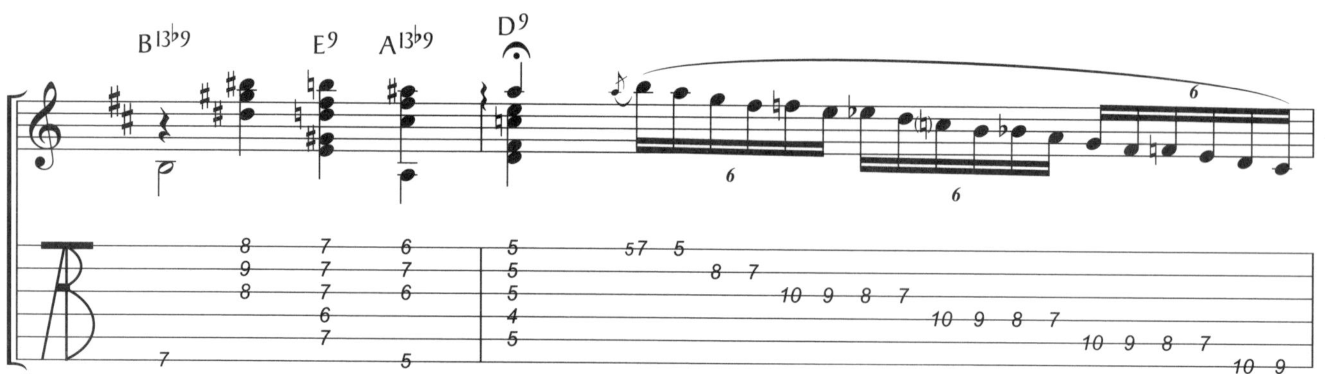
B13♭9
E9
A13♭9
D9

C6/9♯11
3
B13♭9
E9
A13♭9
D6/9♯11

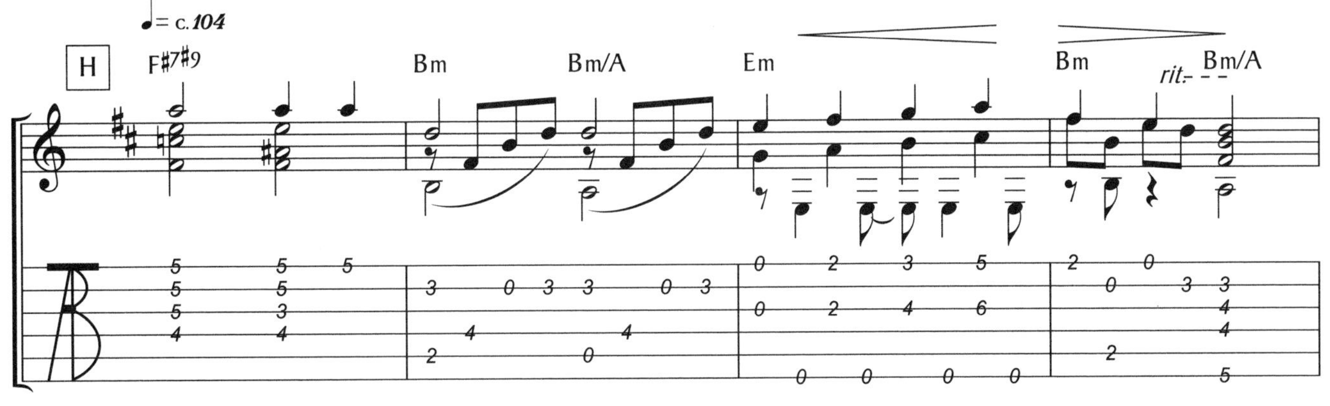
♩= c.104
H
F♯7♭9
Bm
Bm/A
Em
Bm
rit.
Bm/A

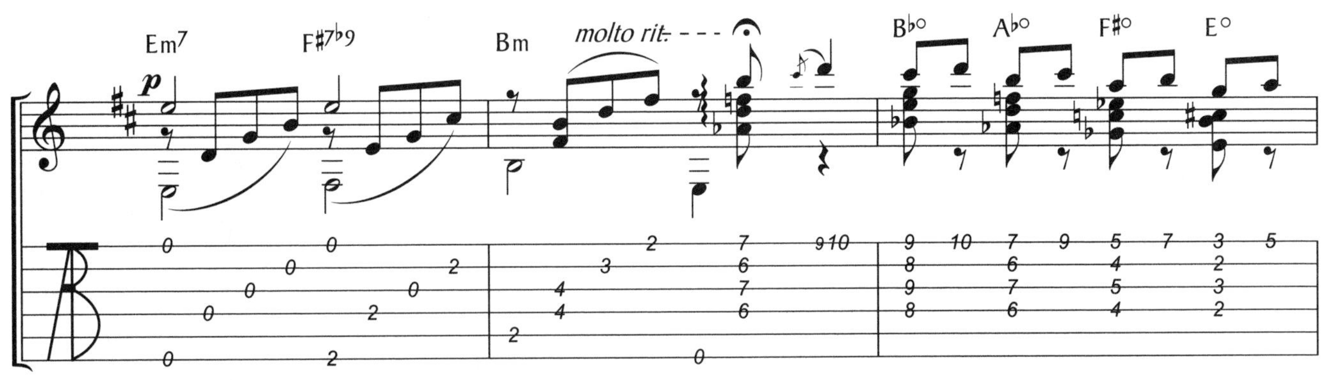
Em7
F♯7♭9
Bm
molto rit.
B♭°
A♭°
F♯°
E°
p

Slowly
E♭°
Em7
F♯7♯5
rit.
Bm
Bm/A
Em9
Bm11
p
pp

artist biographies

Stacy Beyer graduated from college at 19 (and began at the age of 13) with a degree in music. She toured the world as a secular artist and has composed music for television and films. After moving to Nashville at the suggestion of Merle Haggard, she became a staff writer for EMI Music Publishing, with songs recorded by Tracy Byrd, Steve Azar, and many others. She's also had a number one hit in Australia, with a video that played for two years on Australia's CMT. As Jewish music began to emerge as the musical center of her life, Stacy recorded two original Chanukah songs for a Warner Brothers project titled *A Children's Chanukah*. She has performed for 18 years for organizations like B'nai B'rith, Hadassah, NCJW, Youth Camps, JCCs, Jewish Federations, for the URJ Regional and National Biennials, for congregations around the country and many more. In 2006, she was invited by the JCCA to be Vocal Music Artist-in-Residence for the first-ever JCCA ArtsFest program (in Baltimore), created as the artistic "flip side" to the Maccabi Games. Stacy's music has found its way into services, religious schools, community events, and more. Her song, "Keeping the Faith," chosen to be the title cut for a double-CD recording of Jewish music, created by the organzation Voices For Israel, was recorded by 50 female Jewish singers from around the world. Stacy's songs combine singable melodies with catchy grooves, stretching the boundaries while blending with the traditional. Stacy launched her first national tour as a Jewish contemporary recording artist in 2002, giving those who had only heard her recordings an opportunity to experience the raw energy and soulful moments that make Stacy's live performances so memorable. Whether in concert, services or leading songwriting or choir workshops, Stacy's musicianship and dynamic vocal talent continue to capture the attention of her audiences. She is a true and recognizable force in contemporary Jewish music. Stacy and her Grammy-winning co-producer, Gary Dales, are now working on her fourth CD, to be released in 2008.

Steve Dropkin is widely regarded as a major force in Jewish music. He has recorded five albums of original Jewish music. He has performed in England, Israel, and around the United States, including a 2001 performance at Gracie Mansion for Mayor Rudolph Giuliani's Jewish Heritage Celebration. He has been a featured performer at the URJ National Biennial Conventions, the NFTY National Convention, as well at many CAJE conferences. His songs have also been featured on the in-flight listening programs for Tower Airlines.

Debbie Friedman is a singer, songwriter, and guitarist who has recorded 17 albums. Originally influenced by American popular music of the 1960s and 70s, she has been influencing younger singers and songwriters with her own style. Debbie has performed in hundreds of cities in the United States and Canada, Europe, and Israel. Her music is being sung and performed not just in synagogues, but also in churches, schools, camps, and community centers throughout North America and Europe. Debbie's Carnegie Hall concert marked the 25th anniversary of the beginning of her musical career. A native of Minnesota, Debbie, has directed music and singing programs at the University of Judaism in Los Angeles, the University of California at Santa Cruz, Brandeis University, and for almost every major Jewish organization. She received the Bennett H. Walzer Memorial Judaic Arts Award in 1992 and 1994, and the Steven S. Wise Jewish Education Award. Debbie is an honorary lifetime member of the National Federation of Temple Youth. In 1996, Debbie was presented with the prestigious Covenant Foundation Award for her far-reaching impact on Jewish education.

After 25 years of temple and camp song leading, singing in secular bands, giving guitar lessons, and pursuing other career paths, **Sue Horowitz** had finally arrived as a new Jewish singer-songwriter. The former director of education and song leader at Temple Israel in Dover, NH, Sue found a dynamic Jewish song writing partner in Rabbi Lev Baesh. She writes songs that are accessible, user-friendly, and instantly recognizable. Sue can be found leading spirited community singing for people of all ages in the New England region. Her rich voice and warm presence has engaged communities at regional summer camps, Friday night Shabbat services, bar and bat mitzvahs, weekend retreats, concerts, and religious schools.

New York-based singer/songwriter **Mark Aaron James** was raised in Cocoa Beach, Florida, and went to Vanderbilt University in Nashville. It was there that he began his career as a singer/songwriter. A winner of the USA and UNISONG Songwriting Competitions and a finalist at the Kerrville Folk Festival, Mark was voted among the "Best Singer/Songwriters in Greenwich Village" by the Underground Music Organization of New York and "Best Local Songwriter" two years in a row by the Nashville Scene Reader's Poll. Several of his songs have been featured in television shows and movies. His recordings have received glowing reviews from local and national magazines, including *Time Out*, *The Village Voice* and *Performing Songwriter*. He tours regularly throughout the United States and Europe.

Ross M. Levy has burst into the national spotlight with the release of his new album, *Where the Future Lies*. Ross has been involved in the world of Jewish music since his early teen years, and many have enjoyed his energy and spirit at NFTY and congregational events. In recent years, Ross has performed in many areas of the East Coast, appearing in congregations for special Shabbat and Havdalah services as well as leading song sessions and concerts at events sponsored by NFTY and the Union for Reform Judaism. *Where the Future Lies* includes all original music for many of the well-known prayers we use every Shabbat. His style of music is pleasing to all ages, from teens to seniors, and he has received accolades from congregations in Connecticut, Massachusetts, New York, New Jersey, and Pennsylvania. His original style of acoustic rock brings something special to the world of Jewish music. From the catchy pop hit "Im Ein Ani Li Mi Li/Stand Tall" to the beautiful melodies behind "Mi Chamochah/Where The Future Lies," this is music you've got to hear to believe.

Sheldon Low is the newest face in Jewish music, performing rock concerts and leading artist-in-residence weekends in Jewish communities throughout the United States. Sheldon has an undeniable appeal to youth and family audiences, not only as a musician, singer/songwriter, and entertainer, but most important, as a Jewish educator and role model. For the last three summers, Sheldon was a huge hit with teens as he appeared on stage with Jewish rock musician Rick Recht, during Recht's national summer tour, playing at dozens of Jewish summer camps. Sheldon was also recently featured as a head songleader and headliner performing in concert at the 2006 BBYO International Convention. Sheldon is known for regularly featuring local musicians, choirs, and soloists on stage with the band during his concerts, artist-in-residencies, and religious services. Sheldon is Artist in Residence at Barnert Temple in Franklin Lakes, New Jersey. Sheldon's debut album, *On One Foot*, on independent label Jewish Rock Records, was released in June 2006 and includes special guest vocalists and musicians Rick Recht, Beth Schafer, and a choir of BBYO and NFTY teens. Sheldon's song "Heveinu" has already become a major hit for teens across the United States. In October 2007, Sheldon's new children's album, *It's All Challah to Me*, will be distributed nationally. On the road, Sheldon Low brings a wealth of Judaic knowledge to the communities he visits, with extensive experience as a Jewish educator and musician working as a religious school and preschool songleader, youth choir director, youth group songleader, group guitar teacher, Hebrew and b'nai mitzvah tutor, and cantorial soloist.

For the past five years, **Noam Katz** has brought his soulful energy, stirring melodies, and passion for Jewish learning to audiences across the globe, from Uganda to Israel, London to Los Angeles. A longtime songleader at the URJ Eisner and Kutz Camps, Noam remains committed every summer to visiting Jewish camps and training the next generation of songleaders and Jewish role models. During the rest of the year, he and his band travel throughout North America, bringing their exciting world beats and educational programs to children and adults of all ages and denominations. They have performed at the CAJE conference, URJ Biennials, the Limmud Conference in England, the BBYO International Convention, the NFTY Convention, and countless congregations and community centers. Noam has recorded two critically acclaimed albums to date: *Rakia*, a collection of original Shabbat and Havdalah melodies, and *Mirembe, Salaam V'shalom*, an eclectic album with shades of acoustic folk, rock, gospel, reggae and African chant. Noam wrote most of the songs for this latter effort, including his popular setting for "Am Yisrael Chai," in Uganda where he lived and volunteered with the Abayudaya Jewish community in 2003-2004. The experience had a profound impact on Noam's songwriting, infusing it with themes of Jewish unity, tolerance, and social justice. In the summer of 2007, Noam embarked on his latest musical project, teaming up with fellow musician-educator Michael Mason to form Tof B'yad, a groundbreaking musical venture that uses hand-drumming and drum circles to foster teamwork, community, and individual expression. As part of this project, Noam hopes to release an album of all-new, drum-based liturgical music (tentatively titled, *TOF-ilah*) in the fall of 2008. Noam is currently a rabbinical and education student at Hebrew Union College-Jewish Institute of Religion in Los Angeles, where he enjoys the eternal sunshine with his wife Jaime.

Listeners of all ages have enjoyed the Jewish music of singer/songwriter/guitarist **Eric Komar**. With two decades of songleading experience, he performs and teaches at JCCs and Hillels around the country. His peace anthem "Lo Yisa Goi" (from his debut CD *Notes from the Underground*, published in Transcontinental Music's *Shabbat Anthology, Volume 1*), has been used at 9/11 memorial services. Eric ushered in 2007 with the brand new CD *Two Life*. Its featured track, "Justice, Justice," has become a favorite of teens at New York area synagogues. Eric lives in New Jersey with his wife and son. In addition to being a synagogue music specialist, he works in the field of music publishing and teaches guitar.

Mah Tovu comprises Ken Chasen and Josh Zweiback. Whether performing as an acoustic duo, backed by their band (including their producer and collaborator, Gordon Lustig), or joined by their friend and former partner, Steve Brodsky, Mah Tovu's dynamic and moving performances have gained a loyal and enthusiastic following across the country. Their original, contemporary Jewish music is sung in synagogues, schools, and Jewish summer camps nationwide.

Josh Nelson is one of the preeminent performers and producers in modern Jewish music. A multi-instrumentalist and songwriter, Josh's music has been celebrated and integrated into the musical consciousness of congregations, camps, and communities across the United States. His performance style is high-energy and captivating, and his shows consistently leave audiences with a strong feeling of community. Josh has performed over one thousand shows in a variety of venues. Highlights include: international conventions for each of the major youth movements in the United States (NFTY, USY, BBYO), URJ Biennial Conventions, JCCA National Conventions, JCC Maccabi Games, CAJE Conferences, and JCCs across the country.

Dan Nichols is one of the most popular and influential Jewish musicians in North America, performing over 200 concerts a year. His music has become an important part of the Reform Jewish movement, with synagogue youth and clergy alike incorporating it into their curriculum and services. His last two albums have garnered critical acclaim and a legion of growing fans. Songs like "L'takein (The Na Na Song)," "B'tzelem Elohim," "Kehilah Kedoshah," and "My Heart is in the East" are some of the most popular songs in Reform Judaism today.

Rick Recht is one of the top touring artists in Jewish music, playing over 150 concerts each year in the United States and abroad. He has revolutionized and elevated the genre of Jewish rock music as a powerful and effective tool for developing Jewish pride and identity among youth and adults. Rick's impact has been highlighted in many prominent, national and international news organizations including msnbc.com, yahoomusic.com, the *Chicago Tribune*, the *LA Times*, ynetnews.com, and many more. In addition to his six top-selling Jewish albums, Rick has just released *Knockin' Holes in the Darkness*. The brand new CD was recorded live at Hope Presbyterian Church in Memphis, Tennessee on April 19, 2007. *Knockin' Holes* captures the explosive energy of Rick's *Tear Down the Walls* multicultural, interfaith production, featuring Memphis' top gospel and R&B soloists and faith community choirs. *Knockin' Holes in the Darkness* also has three studio bonus tracks including the new single, "Knockin' Holes in the Darkness," featuring Memphis singing powerhouse Karen Brown.

Beth Schafer's skillful songwriting and infectious performances have made her a leading performer of contemporary Jewish music. Both as a solo artist and with her band of seasoned pros, Beth has been featured playing in many diverse venues, from national religious conferences to center court for the halftime show of the Orlando Magic. Beth has now written and co-produced six full-length original recordings. After winning the 2006 American Idol Underground Faith-Based competition, Beth is using her gifts to build bridges between faith communities. It has become her goal to let the music she writes, produces, and performs bring joy, peace and understanding to her ever-expanding audience. When not writing and performing, Beth is the leader of Temple Shir Shalom in Central Florida.

Anchored by thumping beatbox, intricate arrangements, and soulful harmonies, six-man vocal band **Six13** brings an unprecedented style of Jewish music to the stage. With songs that range from hip-hop dance tracks to rock anthems, the members of the New York-based group sound like a full band -- while using nothing but their voices. In 2005, they released the Jewish music community's best-selling album -- the recipient of extensive radio play within that community, two Contemporary A Cappella Recording Award nominations, and selections for four different "best of" compilations -- to critical and commercial acclaim. In 2007, they reinvented Jewish a cappella again with their follow-up, *Encore*, which earned a perfect score from the Recorded A Cappella Review Board. Currently, the group tours nationwide to standing ovations. Recent highlights include the Chabad Telethon, sets for crowds of 30,000+ at Jewish Heritage Day for both the Florida Marlins (Joe Robbie Stadium) and the New York Mets (Shea Stadium), the North American Jewish Choral Festival, New York City's Salute to Israel Parade, a commission by the OU for a national video campaign, and private concerts, affairs and simchas from Oakland to Providence. The boys look forward to continuing to redefine the limitations of the human voice, and churning out some great "new Jewish tunes" in the process.

Peri Smilow is a nationally recognized singer/songwriter, performer, educator and community organizer committed to using the arts as an instrument for social change. Her music has been heard throughout the United States, Canada, England, Singapore, and Israel. Peri has released three recordings of original contemporary Jewish music, including *Songs of Peace*, *Ashrey* and *Peri Smilow & The Freedom Music Project: The Music of Passover and the Civil Rights Movement*, featuring an electrifying 18-voice choir of young black and Jewish singers celebrating the freedom music of their traditions. The Freedom Music Project is the subject of several feature stories broadcast nationally on NBC and ABC TV, National Public Radio's Weekend All Things Considered and internationally on Voice of America radio. *Peri Smilow & The Freedom Music Project* was nominated for Best Gospel Album of the Year (2002) by the Just Plain Folks Music Awards and is now available for replication nationally as *The Freedom Music Project: Concert-in-a-Box*. Peri was an active member of JFTY, is a graduate of Wesleyan University and holds a masters degree in education from Harvard University. She resides just outside of New York City with her husband and their young daughter..